Coming Clean

in the Workplace

Coming Clean

in the Workplace

An **Uncommon Devotional** to Make the
Narco Mindset Work for You

Jorge L. Valdés, Ph.D.

In Collaboration with Anthony Petrucci

Table of Contents

SEVEN STRONG CHARACTER TRAITS:

SEVEN CHARACTER FLAWS:

SEVEN POSITIVE ATTITUDES:

SEVEN STATESOF BEING:

GENERAL SUBJECTS:

FORWARD

In 2005 I found myself in search of help for my oldest son, who was getting involved with drugs. A priest friend told me "Call Jorge. He can tell him all about the harsh reality of drug life." Let's just say that was an understatement! Fifteen years later, we remain great friends and continue to inspire each along the way.

In those years of friendship, I've seen how his past life has not defined him, but rather distilled his character into who he is today − a family man of strong values, integrity and truth. Coming Clean was Jorge's story of coming into the light of truth. Coming Clean in the Workplace continues that journey into our work life, with the awareness that our personal and work lives are both reflections of who we are. To live a truly harmonious life, those values must be in sync to be at peace.

Jorge's life in the fast lane had all the glitz, glamour and riches one could ever want, yet he realized he was unfulfilled and living a double

Jorge L. Valdés, Ph.D. *in Collaboration with Anthony Petrucci*

life. Jorge's experience teaches us that lusting for power, fame and riches ultimately leaves you empty, even though today's world may celebrate those enviable illusions.

Coming Clean in the Workplace challenges business people to come clean and abandon the hypocrisy of duality. He examines the notion that regardless of your spiritual upbringing or cultural influences, business ethics start with a unified truth. Coming Clean in the Workplace means conducting business rooted in the guiding principles of love, honor, fairness, and compassion for others, knowing that those are the lasting rewards of the human spirit.

Robert Farinella
CEO, BlueSky Agency

PURPOSE

Twenty years ago, I had the honor of addressing various members of the US House of Representatives as well as the US Senate. When I finished speaking, a book table was set in the halls of the US Capitol where numerous leaders stood in line for my autograph. After this event, I returned to my hotel room where I was extremely excited to call my wife Sujey and tell her, "Honey, can you believe this that all these leaders were in line for my autograph?"

Quietly she responded, "Do not forget that He who took you up can also bring you down."

I hung up the phone and began to cry. I realized then that our past does not define our present nor our future, and yes, there are consequences to our actions, but if we truly repent from our past actions and seek a new beginning, there is a whole big world that awaits us.

That day I was more than convinced that my immediate future did not lie in being an international speaker and glorying in accolades; my past story could not be my present nor my future story. I had to begin anew, and one day the true story would be told. I would focus on helping my wife building our small carpet cleaning and restoration company, ServiceMaster Total Cleaning.

Jorge L. Valdés, Ph.D. *in Collaboration with Anthony Petrucci*

Sujey and I had bought a small ServiceMaster franchise so that we could support our family. We had learned of the ServiceMaster Company while we were both students at Wheaton College. We admired that a Fortune 500 Company, which held as its number one corporate objective to Honor God in All We Do existed in today's corporate world.

I will never forget that Monday morning when we held our first devotional. My wife, her parents and I held hands and dedicated our company to Honoring God in All We Do. We did not have a job scheduled, nor did we have any idea how we would get any work; however, we were certain that if we lived what we believed, God would add the increase and we would succeed. Four years later, we would gross over $1.4 million dollars in revenue, as our company never failed to have a Monday morning devotional. We have overcome tremendous challenges and experienced great successes.

Since that first morning, Sujey and I struggled to find a devotional that would be applicable to adverse group, which made up our company. We have looked for a devotional that would address the real-life challenges that are faced by a person in the workplace and speak to that person whether they are the boss or the employee. We have struggled to find a devotional that addresses the many topics that face a company, which honors God in all it does, yet is engaged in a business world that adheres to the belief that God has no place in the business world. And we have struggled to find a devotional that is grounded on what we believe to be absolute truths, which are relevant to all our employees, no matter what race, color, or gender they are, or even what form of religious expression they hold to.

Jorge L. Valdés, Ph.D. *in Collaboration with Anthony Petrucci*

This devotional is our offering to an ever-changing market place. It is an offering to those employers who place the interest of their people above those of the company. It is an offering for those employees who truly find the greatest fulfillment in serving others. It is our offering to the God who has blessed our family and employees with so much; the God who has gotten us through immense trials and obstacles. Finally, it is an offering to the God who has provided a faith-friendly company for our employees to work and grow while respecting their believes and identity.

INTRODUCTION

Business ethics is the study of what constitutes right and wrong, or good and bad human conduct in the business world. Business ethics is concerned with moral issues that arise anywhere people and business come together.

When we talk about business ethics, many people laugh about such an idea. Some joke that the term in and of itself is an oxymoron. Yet, for the past two decades, there have been many reports about tragic stories of corporate misconduct. More than a few of these stories have resulted in felony convictions for corporate officers and millions of hard-working Americans losing their entire retirements. These stories should force us not to laugh and joke, but instead to reflect and think more deeply about the nature and purpose of business, and the ethical choices we make on a daily basis, not only in our personal lives, but also in our business lives.

The word ethics comes from the Greek word ethos, which means character or custom. Today, the word ethos is used to refer to the character or attitude of a specific culture or group of people. According to philosophy professor Robert C. Solomon, the etymology of the word ethics suggests its basic concern over individual character, including what it means to be a good individual, and the social rules that govern our conduct, specially the ultimate rules concerning right and wrong, which we call "morality."

In our everyday lives we interchange the words "ethical" and "moral" to describe people and actions we consider being good, and "unethical" and "immoral" to describe actions and people we consider wrong and bad.

We ask: "Where does our moral standard come from?" We must accept the most people have a certain moral code that they explicitly or implicitly accept. Yet, because the moral principles of different individuals in the same society overlap, we must consider a moral code of a society where moral standards are shared in common by its members.

As we consider our early upbringing – the behavior of other people around us, and implied standards of our culture, our own experiences, and our critical reflection on these experiences – it is natural to ask ourselves if, in fact, we can find certain moral principles that are applicable to people of diverse cultures and beliefs.

For the everyday businessperson, what needs to be considered is where these moral principles can be found and what factors influence them. For many, right and wrong, or what philosophers' term "ethical relativism," is a function of what a particular society accepts to be right and wrong. These people subscribe to the theory of "cultural relativism" that suggests that morality is just a function of what a particular society happens to believe. This is the theory that what is right is determined by what a particular culture believes is right. Therefore, what is right in one culture is wrong in another because the only criteria for determining what is right and wrong is the moral system of the society in which the act occurs.

For these people, there is no absolute ethical standard independent of cultural context, no criteria for right and wrong by which to judge the actions of others, other than that of a particular society. In essence, what morality requires is relative to a society.

For other people our morals are a direct by-product of our religious influences. Religion provides its believers with a worldview, part of which involves certain moral instructions, values and commitments. The Jewish and Christian faiths, to name two, present humans as a unique outcome or "product" of a divine intervention; creatures who stand midway between nature and spirit. On the one hand, they are finite and bound to earth, capable of wrongdoing and morally flawed, and on the other hand, capable of transcending nature and realizing infinite possibilities.

Many Americans, due to the influence of Western religions, find their purpose in a serving and loving Higher Being. For the Christian, this is accomplished by emulating the life of Jesus. In Jesus' life, Christians find an expression of the highest virtue – love. They love when they perform selfless acts, develop a keen social conscience and realize that others are creatures of God, and, therefore, very important. In the Jewish faith, and individual serves and loves God through expressions of justice and righteousness.

Our faith then not only becomes a form of worship, but also rescriptions for social relationships. One major example is a mandate found in similar form in every major religion of the world: "Do unto others as you would have them do unto you."

- Good people proceed while considering that what is best for others is best for them. (Hitopadesa, Hinduism).

- Thou shalt love thy neighbor as thyself. (Leviticus 19:18, Judaism)

- Hurt not others with that which pains you. (Udanavarga 5:18, Buddhism)

- What you do not want done to yourself, do not do to others. (Analects 15:23, Confucianism).

Therefore, what is the nature of our morality? Is that nature based on what our religious system of belief says, or is that nature based on what our specific cultural setting has determined to be the standard? If a religious system of beliefs influences the nature of our morality, then the question becomes "whose religion we follow." Even among the Christian faith, there is an enormous difference between beliefs.

If our specific cultural setting defines the nature of our morality, then the question is never ending in that it now becomes who or what in the society sets that standard. And, thus, morality is restricted to time and space. Thus, if morality is defined by our culture, how we do business is geographically dictated.

I suggest that if we accept the premise that humans are born morally flawed and, thus, incapable to do what is right, then morality must be defined by a Higher Power that provides the individual with moral guidance. Without it, the individual has no incentive to be moral. If that Higher Power dictates our morals and we are accountable to Him, how we do business should remain a constant.

This devotional posits that in light of all the scandals in corporate America for decades and what many believe is a decay in our nation's morality, we can extrapolate eternal moral principles not bound to space or time from the Judeo-Christian writings, not as religious writings but as guidelines about morality. These guidelines for our ethical behavior in the workplace can have a tremendous influence on us and on all those around us. The past and present misconduct in the workplace is the result of the suggestion that culture defines what a right and wrong business practice is, and that wrong is only relative to time and place. I humbly disagree.

SEVEN

DEADLY SINS

Jorge L. Valdés, Ph.D. *in Collaboration with Anthony Petrucci*

ONE

GREED

"So the Lord sent Nathan the prophet to tell David this story: There were two men in a certain town. One was rich, and one was poor. The rich man owned many sheep and cattle. The poor man owned nothing but a little lamb he had worked hard to buy. He raised that little lamb, and it grew up with his children. It ate from the man's own plate and drank from his cup. He cuddled it in his arms like a baby daughter. One day a guest arrived at the home of the rich man, but instead of killing a lamb from his own flocks for food, he took the poor man's lamb and killed it and served it to his guest."

(2 Samuel 12: 1-4)

Many of us read the story of David and Bathsheba and cannot conceive how we can become so greedy that we commit such a heinous crime; yet in our daily lives we make choices that have similar consequences. Many of us will not be as bold as to go ahead and commit murder, but the scars we leave on others' lives, as they become victims of our greed, are traumatic, deadly and can have eternal consequences. In a materialistic world, it is easy to lose focus on the impact that greed not only has on us, but also on others.

Greed is the desire to have more, to acquire whatever one can get his/her hands on, to amass without any correlation to one's own specific

Jorge L. Valdés, Ph.D. *in Collaboration with Anthony Petrucci*

needs or those of others. A greedy person is confused about life; a greedy person does not realize that the meaning to life and the satisfaction of living a purposeful life has no correlation to material possessions. We go through life stepping over anyone who gets in our way in our climb to that summit where we believe all our problems will disappear and we will find fulfillment for our lives. However, the saddest part of reaching the summit is that, if we ever get there, we find out that what we thought was there is actually not there.

It is extremely sad how the false assumption that material possessions will fill the emptiness within us drives millions of honest people to make horrific choices. We lie to ourselves and others, and we work so hard to amass things that society has convinced us that, once we have them, we will then finally be happy. We lose focus of what really matters and what truly fills the emptiness within us. We sacrifice our health and abandon our loved ones only to spend all the wealth we have to either recoup our health or save our loved ones from addictions they endure as a result of our abandonment.

If we look at David as a murderer and correlate this to God's statement that David was a man after God's own heart, we realize that not only does God love those whom society has condemned but that there was something unique about David that allowed God to look beyond the criminal. Is it perhaps that David lived a transparent life of repentance and contrition, not only before others, but most importantly before God? As humans in a fallen world, we will fall into greed and hurt others as a result of our greed. This is to be understood and not to

20

be accepted. When we realize that we have committed an act of greed, we must immediately come clean about it.

Lord, search my heart. May I gain a greater awareness of my own tendency toward greed.

MEDITATION: Take an inventory of your life as it relates to greed.

Jorge L. Valdés, Ph.D. *in Collaboration with Anthony Petrucci*

TWO

PRIDE

"While he was still speaking these words, a voice called down from heaven, O King Nebuchadnezzar, this message is for you! You are no longer ruler of this kingdom. You will be driven from human society. You will live in the fields with the wild animals, and you will eat grass like a cow. Seven periods of time will pass while you live this way, until you learn that the Most High rules over the kingdoms of the world and gives them to anyone he chooses. That very same hour the prophecy was fulfilled, and Nebuchadnezzar was driven from human society." (Daniel 4: 30-33)

Nebuchadnezzar II ruled Babylonia from 605 to 562 B.C. He was the most powerful and longest reigning king of the Neo-Babylonian (625-539 B.C.) period. He brought the city of Babylon and the southern Mesopotamian state of Babylonia to the pinnacle of their power and prosperity. Yet, with one quick blow, God brought him all the way down. Pride truly did come before a fall.

If we ponder over the seven deadly sins, most of us would have to admit that pride is not only the most subtle of them but is probably the one we most struggle with. From the beginning of time, we find man on a journey to be like God and to strive for positions of influence and

Jorge L. Valdés, Ph.D. *in Collaboration with Anthony Petrucci*

power. If we search deeply within our souls, we find that the root of the search for power is pride. Humans are proud people who will not hesitate a second to allow the world to see just how great we are.

When compared to Nebuchadnezzar, we have peace that we will never be a king, nor will we ever build such a great empire, and truthfully so. Yet, the sin of pride is relevant to where we are in life. For most in the workplace, pride sneaks in as a promotion, or a great sales job, or in daily numbers we have met. In our families, pride manifests itself through materialism. It is exemplified in the old adage: "keeping up with the Jones." As humans, we are proud of our achievements in the workplace and in our homes. We are proud of our jobs and our homes. We are proud of our children and of their academic and sports accolades. And in all truth, we should be proud of these achievements.

Therefore, if this is so, where is the problem and where is the sin? The sin of pride is not the fact that, as humans, we prosper or achieve great things. The sin lies in who gets the credit, and how we reveal those achievements to others. For people of faith, it is good to let the world know that we prosper as we live a life above reproach; that our children are doing great in school and perhaps that they are great athletes. The mystery lies in finding that fine line that takes pride from a manifestation of God's providence in our lives to a sinful boast about how great we think we are. To have a clear perspective where this line lies, we must remain humble and seek God's daily guidance.

Jorge L. Valdés, Ph.D. *in Collaboration with Anthony Petrucci*

Lord, help me to remain humble before you and others, as I boast in only YOU!

MEDITATION: Seeking God's guidance daily fosters a clear perspective on where the line is drawn between pride and being blessed. No matter how "good" it may look or feel in the moment, it is a spiritual law that pride comes before a fall.

Jorge L. Valdés, Ph.D. *in Collaboration with Anthony Petrucci*

THREE

ENVY

"There are six things the Lord hates - no, seven things he detests: haughty eyes, a lying tongue, hands that kill the innocent, a heart that plots evil, feet that race to wrong, a false witness who pours out lies, a person who sows discord among brothers." (Proverbs 6: 16-19)

The Judeo-Christian Scriptures tell us about many envious people. We find King Saul trying to kill David because of envy; Joseph's brothers sell him as a slave because of envy, and Cain kills Abel because of envy, among other things. How many people in the Bible can you imagine exhibited haughty eyes? Jezebel, Haman, Nebuchadnezzar, Saul (before he became Paul on the road to Damascus), the religious Pharisees and, of course, Satan himself.

Proverbs 6 points to things that the Lord hates, yet not one of the "seven things" (characteristics) mention the word "envy." However, if we pause for a moment and see all the stories that tell about someone being envious of someone else throughout the Scriptures, then what we find is that every one of the things the Lord has mentioned as things He hates are manifested in the envious individual.

Jorge L. Valdés, Ph.D. *in Collaboration with Anthony Petrucci*

It is extremely sad to see how often we profess to be a "religious person of faith," and yet our behavior exemplifies every single attribute that is despised by the Lord. We find that, when we are jealous of another co-worker, we have a tendency to lie about them; we look at them with haughty eyes; we plan evil in our hearts and spend a great amount of time sowing discord. Why?

The answer is complex and, if we ask psychologists, they will most likely give us a million reasons. But if we allow the biblical stories of envy enlighten us, we find that people who are envious are those that are not grounded in God's Word, and they place themselves above others. We find individuals whose identities are not grounded in the truth of God's Word. And, therefore, others are insignificant -- outside of whatever role they may play in furthering that individual's mission.

It was hard for the apostles to understand the Messiah whom Jesus was portraying. After all, they were sure that their messiah would come in the line of David, a warrior who would destroy all who had abused them. Therefore, how could their Davidic messiah say that He was not the warrior who would lead them into battle and victory, but instead He was the "suffering servant" described in the book of Isaiah? Jesus would describe the ultimate being as he who would lay down his life for others. If we find our identity grounded in God's Word and not in our self-seeking attitudes, then we would not envy others, but instead we'd respect them and love them above ourselves.

Jorge L. Valdés, Ph.D. *in Collaboration with Anthony Petrucci*

Lord, cleanse my heart of the self-centeredness and insecurity that spur envy and all the ugliness it generates, while helping me to love others selflessly.

MEDITATION: How often do we place others above ourselves? How willing are we to surrender our arrogance to God in exchange for a humble heart, which is a heart reshaped into the image of the Lord's own heart?

Jorge L. Valdés, Ph.D. *in Collaboration with Anthony Petrucci*

FOUR

GLUTTONY

"Destruction is certain for the land whose king is a child and whose leaders feast in the morning. Happy is the land whose king is a nobleman and whose leaders feast only to gain strength for their work, not to get drunk." *(Ecclesiastes 10: 16-17)*

In the Nicene and Post-Nicene Fathers Second Series Vol. XI, the founding church fathers struggled with the concept of gluttony. To them, gluttony, or bodily lusts, could not be extinguished except by rooting out vice from one's life. "For it is impossibility that the fiery motions of the body can be extinguished, before the incentives of the other chief vices. . . Gluttony, that is the desire of the palate, against which our first battle is. He then will never be able to check the motions of a burning lust, who cannot restrain the desires of the appetite."

When we think about gluttony, we associate it with overeating or perhaps we correlate it with a need to diet. One look at all diet books being written and one can see that gluttony expressed in overeating is a major concern of our modern society. But if we search deeper, as the

Jorge L. Valdés, Ph.D. *in Collaboration with Anthony Petrucci*

Nicene and Post-Nicene writer did, we find that overeating is just another manifestation of a greater evil.

Gluttony is a bodily lust manifested in many vices, indeed. It amazes me how many times religious people judge those who drink alcohol and yet fail to see how overweight they are. We are quick to point out the sins of others while failing to see those which haunt us.

I often wonder about the existence of a tremendous world hunger problem and how others created by the same God as ours are dying because of hunger, but in America it seems that the entire population is on a diet. To me, the answer lies in the vices of greed, avarice, pride and many others. We profess to be people of faith who love others as we love ourselves, but indeed this is not true. We love ourselves first and many times only.

We care for others as long as that care does not impose on our lives. We provide out of our excess and not out of our love. We love our neighbor only when that neighbor fits our mold. We do all this and more because of the sin of gluttony. Gluttony is not relegated to overeating, but is also expressed in power, pride and lust.

Lord, give me wisdom to be able to eliminate gluttony from my life.

MEDITATION: Can you think of ways in which gluttony manifests itself in your life?

Jorge L. Valdés, Ph.D. *in Collaboration with Anthony Petrucci*

FIVE

LUST

"So then, since Christ suffered physical pain, you must arm yourselves with the same attitude he had, and be ready to suffer, too. For if you are willing to suffer for Christ, you have decided to stop sinning.

And you won't spend the rest of your life chasing after evil desires, but you will be anxious to do the will of God. You have had enough in the past of the evil things that godless people enjoy—their immoralityand lust, their feasting and drunkenness and wild parties, and their terrible worship of idols."

(I Peter 4: 1-3)

Contrary to power, which most people desire but most likely will never attain, lust is a sin that afflicts all of humanity, without respect of person. As a result of our sexual lusts, pornography has taken an immense hold on our society. Because we lust after our neighbor's possessions, we work so hard and so long that we abandon the greatest gift God has given us: our children and our families.

It is very interesting that the Greek word for lust *epithymia* is the same word used by many of the biblical writers to express any strong desire. Luke uses the word *epithymia* to refer to an intense and pure desire of Christ (Luke. 22:15). Paul uses *epithymia* in his letter to the

Jorge L. Valdés, Ph.D. *in Collaboration with Anthony Petrucci*

Philippians to express his desire to be with Christ, and in his letter to the church at Thessalonica to express his longing to see his converts (1 Thessalonians 2:17).

How can a word in one instance express a good desire and in another express a deadly sin? The answer I believe lies in our view of sin. In his devotional, "My Outmost for His Highest," Oswald Chambers titles the June 23rd devotional "Acquaintance with Grief." In it, he posits, "At the beginning of life we do not reconcile ourselves to the fact of sin. We take a rational view of life and say that a man by controlling his instincts, and by educating himself, can produce a life which will slowly evolve into the life of God."

For Chambers, sin has a way of making all things wild and not rational. "We have to recognize that sin is a fact, not a defect; sin is red-handed mutiny against God. Either God or sin must die in my life."

Lust is the acceptance of sin in our lives and in our workplace as a human defect which we cannot do anything about. However, we must see lust as a moral choice to be avoided, which, if not, has the power to destroy us. When we look upon lust in the manner in which Luke, Paul and many other biblical writers look at it, we can appropriate its power for our lives.

Lord, allow me to lust after You and not the world. I need Your power to overcome the temptations that confront me to stir up lust. Help me to choose real love (Your love, Lord), instead of lust.

Jorge L. Valdés, Ph.D. *in Collaboration with Anthony Petrucci*

MEDITATION: When you think of the word "lust," what comes to your mind? If sin, then ask God to give you a lust (a strong desire) for His Word. In addition, what do you think are the differences between lust and pure love?

SIX

ANGER

"And don't sin by letting anger gain control over you. Don't let the sun go down while you are still angry, for anger gives a mighty foothold to the Devil." *(Ephesians 4: 26-27)*

The Apostle Paul recognizes that human beings will get angry; he does not pass judgment on anger in and of itself, but what impact it has on our lives. What concerned Paul is the effect that anger has on people as it gets the best of them.

The longer we allow anger to consume us, the greater the danger that it will leave lasting scars. As we look around our workplaces and our lives, it almost seems that everyone is angry about one thing or another. In our workplace, our first reaction when something goes wrong is to get angry and do and say things that later we wish we could take back.

Yet, words once uttered are impossible to retract. It is extremely sad that in our workplace today the reason 70 percent of employees leave their jobs is because they are not appreciated, as it is often expressed in anger. We are so conditioned to focus on us and our needs that, when they are not met, we do not search within us to find what part we play in it, but we lash out at others, as if the burst of anger frees us from our pain. Expressed anger is the visible evidence of our internal pain. When anger goes uncontrolled, many victims lie in our path. We lash out at our associates, friends and family; no one is exempt.

Many of us have spent thousands of dollars in therapy to address the impact words have on our lives. We heal quickly from physical abuse, yet verbal abuse leaves lasting scars often manifested in many addictions. Yet, there is a positive anger that the Scriptures call "righteous indignation." This kind of anger is when people of faith despise sin with great passion that, when we see others being wronged, it pains to the point of compelling us to action.

As a society, we have become complacent that it seems we are immune to sin. We are so consumed with ourselves and what is in it for me that others have become a commodity and, thus, when we get angry and attack them, it does not worry us what impact those words will have on them.

We must focus on shifting our anger from one which attacks others to one of righteous indignation. We must work hard at controlling our anger so that it will not consume our lives and the lives of those we love. When we get angry, we must repent and come clean with those whom we have hurt. We must look upon our anger as a weakness that needs to be corrected and not one that we are comfortable living with.

Jorge L. Valdés, Ph.D. *in Collaboration with Anthony Petrucci*

Lord, help me to control my anger and give me conviction to come clean about it.

MEDITATION: When you get angry, how does it make you feel about yourself afterwards? When have you gotten angry because you were first hurt emotionally?

Jorge L. Valdés, Ph.D. *in Collaboration with Anthony Petrucci*

SEVEN
LAZINESS

"The lazy person is full of excuses, saying, 'I can't go outside because there might be a lion on the road! Yes, I'm sure there's a lion out there!' As a doorturns back and forth on its hinges, so the lazy person turns over in bed. Some people are so lazy that they won't lift a finger to feed themselves. Lazy people consider themselves smarter than seven wise counselors." (Proverbs 23: 13-16)

It is ironic that when we look at people who are lazy, often times we believe that they have no motivation or drive to succeed and achieve things in life. We wonder how some fellow co-workers are so lazy and not motivated like ourselves.

Or we wonder why our children are lazy and simply do not care about things, especially like us. The irony to the above lies is that often the lazy person is extremely confident in his distorted form of wisdom and his rationale for his actions.

Some tend to believe: "why work so hard when at the end the government will take my earnings?" Others suggest that when we work

Jorge L. Valdés, Ph.D. *in Collaboration with Anthony Petrucci*

so hard, we are buying into some sort of capitalistic idea that at the end all it achieves is to suppress people and drive people into debt.

Many times, those who subscribe to these propositions are right. Some people are lazy because they lack purpose and meaning to their lives. A lazy person cannot look beyond the moment in time where they stand. They wake up and see today no different than tomorrow; they see today as another routine that they have mastered.

They will do as little as it is necessary to basically achieve the same as yesterday. A lazy person cannot grasp any significance in doing more than what is absolutely necessary. The other side of the coin is the workaholic who sacrifices health and family for riches -- only to spend that wealth in a futile attempt to recoup that health and mend the family.

The "hard worker"—as that person often labels themselves—is only motivated by how much he/she has accumulated or achieved. They are so driven by that motivation that they fail to see tomorrow.

I want to suggest that finding balance is the key to being able to see beyond today. It's a balance that motivates us to be all that we were created to be; to provide the best we are able for our loved ones without abandoning them; to help achieve the goals set forth by our employer while carrying our load; and to please our Creator. When we find the balance that makes us as productive as we should be, while providing

Jorge L. Valdés, Ph.D. *in Collaboration with Anthony Petrucci*

a healthy and safe place for our loved ones, we become an example for others and ours.

Lord, allow me to be all that you created me to be, and help me not to be so driven that I lose all that that is dear to me.

MEDITATION: How can we balance our lives so that we are neither lazy nor over-achievers?

Jorge L. Valdés, Ph.D. *in Collaboration with Anthony Petrucci*

SEVEN

BEATITUDES

Jorge L. Valdés, Ph.D. *in Collaboration with Anthony Petrucci*

EIGHT

MERCIFUL

"The Lord our God is merciful and forgiving, even though we have rebelled against him." (Daniel 9:9)

God extends his mercy to us, not because we deserve it, but because He is full of mercy. Now, in the 21st century, one wonders what is the value of the mercy of a "higher power" that may simply allow things to randomly happen in the world or keeps out of touch with daily realities that burden human beings. Why would anyone need the "mercy" of God? And what good is it, other than getting into heaven after one passes away from this world?

If you were to examine the "average" acts of human beings and compare them to what the Bible says is good, righteous, holy, beautiful and pure, then one cannot come to any other conclusion than the fact that people have rebelled against God; we have broken His laws and we have done the opposite of what His Word says is the godly way (the perfect way).

Rebelling against God does not necessarily have to be desecrating a church or shaking your fist at the sky, like the historic Russian leader

Jorge L. Valdés, Ph.D. *in Collaboration with Anthony Petrucci*

Joseph Stalin did seconds before he died decades ago in an apparent last defiant expression against God – the same God whom Stalin supposedly did not believe even existed.

Rebellion against God starts with human pride and getting your own way, apart from God's purposes. Rebellion is ignoring what God says to do and living a selfish life that defines its own standard of "good." Because we have all fallen short of God's standard of perfection, we either need to be judged or we need a "judge" to have mercy on us, giving us what we don't deserve.

Is it better to be in the hands of an angry God or a merciful and forgiving God? Since we have all broken His laws, it is beneficial to all of us for God to be merciful and forgiving. Even when we blow it and make mistakes, we can go to Him, admit our mistake and ask for forgiveness, just as we would do in a relationship with anyone we care about. According to the Scriptures, God is quick to forgive and, unlike most people, totally forget your mistakes. God is the God of second chances.

This is a beautiful model for us to learn how authentic, valued-based leadership extends mercy to people in business. Just as God is merciful, we reflect Him when we are merciful to our employees and partners. We do not need to be "perfectionists" who are taskmasters pointing out everyone's faults and punishing people for mistakes. When you care about your colleagues or your team, you are quick to show them mercy, the same way you'd appreciate it if people are merciful to you when you make mistakes – and we all make mistakes at one time or another.

Jorge L. Valdés, Ph.D. *in Collaboration with Anthony Petrucci*

Lord, make me merciful toward other people, recognizing that I have a tendency to hold them to my standards, just as you hold me to Your standards as Creator. May I increase my leadership skills by demonstrating mercy to others in the workplace and helping others grow through their mistakes.

MEDITATION: To whom have you been merciful recently? Can you also think of a time when you reacted in anger and outrage, but could have been merciful? How would a merciful response have changed the outcome?

Jorge L. Valdés, Ph.D. *in Collaboration with Anthony Petrucci*

NINE

PEACE

"Don't worry about anything; instead, pray about everything. Tell God what you need, and thank him for all he has done. If you do this, you will experience God's peace, which is far more wonderful than the human mind can understand." (Philippians 4:6-7)

As I look over the list of all devotional topics, I have decided today to write on peace, hoping that as I research the topic and I pray for the wisdom to write, somehow the process will minister to me in the face of all the struggles we face daily. I struggle with the consequences of the choices I made when I searched for peace in material possession. I struggle with the desire to find peace in a world that surrounds me with chaos. And, most of all, I struggle to find peace in my faith, my God.

I know that for those of us who attempt to live our lives by faith, it provides guidelines and admonitions that once implemented produce peace. This is easier said than done. We pray; we worship and we make our faith the essence of our lives, yet problems never cease to exist. I remember when I struggled with finding peace to write when I saw my wife struggle with cash flow issues in the company that supported me to be in ministry. In essence, at times it seems almost impossible to

43

find peace when there are thousands of dollars in payroll to meet every Friday.

Our struggles in the workplace are all relevant. So how do we find peace when there seems to be none in sight? To me, it is almost the same a playing "Monday morning quarterback." I look back through my life and meditate on all the numerous times when I felt a sense of desperation at what seemed like an insurmountable challenge. Nonetheless, my faith in my God, who has not ever abandoned me, would be present and I would overcome and go on to live another day.

My human mind cannot understand how it all works, nor can it understand why it always seems as if my God takes me to that last second; nonetheless, He always comes through. Yet, even when it seems that there is no hope and we fail to see any light outside of the tunnel, He provides a peace that is beyond our rational understanding.

The greatest evidence of this peace was manifested the day I buried my father. I could not conceive how I could ever be able to go through life without him, but the day I buried him I had a peace I never experienced before that assured me that all would be alright and that we would be reunited again.

The peace that the temporal world provides never lasts and is in a constant flux. Many factors influence it: the economy, our intelligence or, at times, our manipulative abilities. Yet, God's peace that surmounts all understanding is only dependent on our dependency on Him. The economy does not affect it. It is dependent on confessing our needs, and our frailties and believing that He who has brought us this far will never abandons us.

Lord, strengthen me to believe that He who promised is capable of fulfilling that promise. I believe in who You are and that You love me enough to stay true to Your Word.

MEDITATION: How often do you reflect on what God has done for you? Is your peace dependent on Him or you or something else, such as the economy or other outward circumstances?

Jorge L. Valdés, Ph.D. *in Collaboration with Anthony Petrucci*

TEN

PERSECUTION

"Others, like seed sown on rocky places, hear the word and at once receive it with joy. But since they have no root, they last only a short time. When trouble or persecution comes because of the word, they quickly fall away." (Mark 4:16-18)

When two people are married, it can seem "fun" and "cheery" and "light-hearted" in the early days of the marriage, but, inevitably, challenges come, such as disagreements, unexpected financial burdens, selfish intentions and other people saying negative things. When the married couple have the deep "roots" of a firm commitment, good communication, a method of conflict resolution and genuine respect for one another – qualities that have been built up with work over a period of time – you can see that the marriage has "roots" to help them weather the "storm" of challenges.

In a similar way, when you are in relationship with God and have a covenant (stronger than a commitment) with the Lord, it can seem fun in the beginning when God is answering your prayers and has given you an inner peace you have never experienced before. You could feel

Jorge L. Valdés, Ph.D. *in Collaboration with Anthony Petrucci*

like God is your spiritual vending machine to get stuff that you want. You will continue to go to church, practice your "faith" and read the Bible as long as God keeps you living a trouble-free life.

But as soon as trouble comes to you, you abandon God. You are back to your old ways, which are self-centered, prideful and carnal. In this case, there are no "roots" to your faith. God was simply a convenience to get things you want or to avoid something that would cause you pain, but the persecution (trouble) reveals that you are not committed to God or a godly lifestyle. Your faith is weak and you are overcome by doubts about God, as if He had let you down.

The truth is that you don't really know your level of commitment to someone or something until trouble (persecution) comes. And then when you take a stand to remain faithful, despite the persecution, then your faith is strengthened and you can face the adversities of life with greater agility and move in the power of the Spirit. But you need to develop "roots" through persevering in the hard times.

Persecution does not necessarily mean something bad. It doesn't translate into "poor me" if other people are criticizing you, hounding you, threatening you or verbally trying to destroy you – essentially, persecuting you. God can use persecution to toughen up your resolve, make you "battle tested" for bigger assignments in the future, and prove to the world that you can confront evil with good.

Lord, give me your perspective about persecution, so that I may be patient through it and allow you to use persecution, big and small, to sharpen and strengthen my commitment to your plan for my life.

MEDITATION: Can you think of times when you felt persecuted, such as kids picking on you when you were young, or a boss picking on you, or other people making fun of you for going to church or refusing to do drugs?

Jorge L. Valdés, Ph.D. *in Collaboration with Anthony Petrucci*

ELEVEN

DEPENDENCE

"Be strong and very courageous! Obey all the laws Moses gave you. Do not turn away from them, and you will be successful in everything you do. Study this Book of the Law continually. Mediate on it day and night so you may be sure to obey all that is written it. Only then will you succeed."

(Joshua 1: 7-8)

It is a common presupposition that God has no place in the business world. We are tolerant of people who practice any form of religion on Sunday, but that religious expression has to be confined to the church and is not brought to work on Monday morning. Yet, the God, who led Joshua into Canaan and was now preparing him to build a great nation, was very clear in what he expected of Joshua day and night.

To add validity to the above, we often tell others that we are of a set religion, yet, outside of this verbal expression, there is no evidence in our actions. It is hard for us to hold onto an absolute truth. It is easier to suggest that perhaps what God was instructing Joshua was appropriate thousands of years ago, but not in our constantly changing world. We have to continually change if we are to keep up with the workplace.

49

I suggest that many of the things written thousands of years ago were only relevant for that society in that time and place in our history. Many of the Judeo-Christian writings were composed to address specific problems occurring during the times and communities of the writers. Yet, we must differentiate between what was an admonition for a certain time and a timeless principle. Then we can differentiate between those timeless writings that have principles and admonitions from those bound to time or culture.

To meditate on these writings day and night does not mean that we spend every second of our existence reading them; if we do this, we have no time to work; all we would do is read. What this verse speaks to me is that, as I go through my day, facing the many challenges I face daily, I reach back to these timeless principles for guidance set forth in these writings; then I will find success, not in some of the things I do, but in all the things I do. Yet, how can I or anyone else reach out to these eternal principles if I have no knowledge that they exist?

Lord, give me a hunger for your Word, and, when in doubt, allow me to reach for it as a guiding post for my life. Teach me Your timeless principles that are as relevant today as they were thousands of years ago. You are the same today as You were back then.

MEDITATION: How many of these timeless principles found in the Judeo-Christian writings do you know? When in doubt, where can you find them?

Jorge L. Valdés, Ph.D. *in Collaboration with Anthony Petrucci*

TWELVE

MOURNING

"I say to God my Rock, "Why have you forgotten me? Why must I go about mourning, oppressed by the enemy?" (Psalm 42:9)

King David, whom the Bible described as 'a man after God's own heart," felt at times that God had forgotten him. He went around feeling down and sorrowful, as if he were in mourning. If your company misses a quarterly earning or misses out on a big contract or is struggling to pay next week's payroll, you may also feel as if you are in mourning.

We first think of the word "mourning" as to mean "grieving" the loss of a loved one. But so many other things in life can make you feel as if you have entered a season of "mourning" – a loss of something. In the business world, it could be the loss of a job, the loss of a business, the loss of major revenue, or the loss of a business partnership. It could send you into heavy-laden feelings, weighing you down.

You could feel like everyone has forgotten you – God, your customers, the marketplace, your employees and your friends. Like with David, your "enemies" may be oppressing you, such as creditors, competitors or critics. The feelings of being "oppressed" can be overwhelming. So you find yourself asking the poignant question: "Why?"

Why are you suffering? Why are you feeling down? Why have you been seemingly forgotten? Why do you feel oppressed, stressed or worn down? David called God his "Rock." Had God forgotten David? If we take everything the Scriptures say about God, then we know that God had not forgotten about David. But what we glean from the verse is that a person can believe in God, trust his/her God and feel strongly that faith is the connection to a rock of stability, but still feel down, negative, beaten up and scared.

For one, it shows that emotions are not trustworthy because they are responding to outward circumstances. There are times when you, as a leader or a businessperson, need to trust your gut and your vision for the future, refusing to allow the perceptions of the "enemy" coming down on you to stop you from moving forward. There may also be some seasons when you feel like you are mourning the loss of something. But treat it this way: it's only for a season; it's temporary. Mourning may last all night, like dark clouds with rumbling thunder, but rays of light (hope for your business or livelihood) and a break in the clouds (circumstances) come in the morning. Your prayers become declarations over yourself, reminding yourself that you are not forgotten.

Lord, help me to endure any season of mourning when I need to grieve the loss of something or someone, but help me also to move on and see the light of shifting circumstances to deliver new hope.

MEDITATION: How have you mourned the loss of something in the business world or academic world? What positive thing helped you to come out of the season of mourning in the past?

Jorge L. Valdés, Ph.D. *in Collaboration with Anthony Petrucci*

THIRTEEN
GENTLE / MEEK

"God blesses those who are gentle and lowly, for the whole earth will belong to them." (NLT) "Blessed are the meek: for they shall inherit the earth." (NAS) (Matthew 5:5)

In today's work environment, where any sign of kindness and humility is construed as weakness, a statement that urges one to be gentle and meek becomes a serious concern. Yet, Jesus instructs His followers to be just that: gentle, lowly, meek. It is no wonder that there was no way they could understand Him. After all, if His followers are to usher in the Kingdom of God and in their eyes overthrow the Roman Empire, then how could their king, leader, and deliverer instruct them to be meek and lowly?

The Bible tells us that many left Him as it did not make any sense to them, and it does not make sense to us today. It does not make sense if we buy into a pleasure-driven world where the most important element becomes me. It does not make sense if we view humans as a product/commodity and not as a unique gift from God. It does not make sense if we believe that serving others is a state of servitude to be

Jorge L. Valdés, Ph.D. *in Collaboration with Anthony Petrucci*

avoided at all cost. If all this does not make any sense, then how do we make sense of this verse and enjoy its blessing?

Jesus was not going to be the Davidic Messiah that was going to overthrow the Roman Empire by force as the Jewish nation expected and wanted to be part of. For Jesus, the true Kingdom of God was going to be exemplified through love. What greater expression of love is there than when we lay our lives down for a friend? True fulfillment does not exist when we take others for granted and place ourselves above all; true fulfillment is when we place others above "self" -- even to the point of dying for others. When others become more important than us, then we can experience a state of being meek and lowly and then life is no longer self-centered and empty, but purposeful and significant.

When life has purpose, all obstacles can be overcome. When life is meaningless, then all become insurmountable. For people of faith, meekness is based on humility, not a natural quality, but an outgrowth of a renewed nature; whereas, for others the word implies condescension. When God is the center of our lives, our love for others is manifested as an outgrowth of a spiritual relation to God.

Lord, allow me to be meek and find real meaning in serving others.

MEDITATION: What does being meek mean to you? Can you accept Jesus teaching on this subject?

FORTEEN

HUNGRY FOR JUSTICE

"Justice - do you rulers know the meaning of the word? Do you judge the people fairly?" (Psalm 58: 1-5)

Justice is a topic that most of the time we look at it as one-sided. We are quick to point out injustices when others wrong us; this is especially true in the workplace. We wonder how "just" it is when we see our bosses prosper and we work so hard without being properly compensated or even thanked. As a community of faith, we wonder how just can God be when the wicked prosper, yet good moral, hard-working people of faith struggle so hard (Psalm 73). To find our answers, we need to see what justice to God is.

Most human beings want to be rewarded for good deeds, but definitely do not want to suffer for the bad choices they make. Yet, God's justice demands that, if right is to be compensated, wrong must be punished. We must acknowledge that God is not just if He only rewards good choices and ignores bad choices. No group of godly men was more concerned for justice than the Founding Fathers when they wrote the Declaration of Independence.

Jorge L. Valdés, Ph.D. *in Collaboration with Anthony Petrucci*

In August 17, 1858, honoring the Founding Fathers of the United States, Abraham Lincoln wrote:

"Wise statesmen they were, they knew the tendency of prosperity to breed tyrants, and so they established these great self-evident truths, that when in the distant future some man, some faction, some interest, should set up the doctrine that none but rich men, or none but white men, were entitled to life, liberty and the pursuit of happiness, their posterity might look up again to the Declaration of Independence. . . so that truth, and justice, and mercy, and all the humane and Christian virtues might not be extinguished from the land."

It is amazing how more than two hundred years ago these great men of faith knew that, if left unchecked, humanity had a tendency to distort justice. Not only did they know that people would distort justice for self-gratifying reasons, but they also they made provisions for posterity to provide a just society where all people would be provided the same opportunities to live out the American dream that would make us a very distinct and blessed nation.

As we look at the 21st century landscape, we are hard to find one man of the caliber of those who penned the Declaration of Independence. Could there be a direct correlation between a society whose scholarly curriculum was 90 percent based on moral character and the Bible and only 10 percent on math? Think of such visionary leaders as Jefferson, Washington, Adams and Franklin. Our world today is very different than the world of 1776. It's a self-centered world that is not concerned with what is just for all, a world that has lost sight

Jorge L. Valdés, Ph.D. *in Collaboration with Anthony Petrucci*

of the fact that it is our religious foundation created by a just God that makes sure that justice can prevail; a foundation that sees all human beings as a precious creation and not a commodity.

Lord, please help me to seek justice as you have been just with me.

MEDITATION: Would the people who know you say that you are a just person?

SEVEN

EFFECTIVE

HABITS

Jorge L. Valdés, Ph.D. *in Collaboration with Anthony Petrucci*

FIFTEEN

PROACTIVE

Jesus said, "I am not referring to all of you; I know those I have chosen. But this is to fulfill this passage of Scripture: 'He who shared my bread has turned against me.' I am telling you now before it happens, so that when it does happen you will believe that I am who I am." (John 13:17-19)

Jesus Christ was proactive about predicting the betrayal that would propel him to the Cross of Calvary. It was what we commonly call "the last supper" for Jesus and his 12 disciples. He called out Judas proactively, but you should notice that it was all part of the bigger plan. Jesus, who was proactively taking on the problem of humanity's sin nature (separation from God), did not wait for others to react to what ended up happening; He called it out and indicated that it would be evidence of who He really is.

There is power in being proactive. In business, rather than waiting for a problem to solve itself (which it rarely does), you can take a page out of Jesus' playbook and proactively address the problem. But what is an even greater level of business acumen and leadership is to acknowledge proactively that there will be problems; however, those

Jorge L. Valdés, Ph.D. *in Collaboration with Anthony Petrucci*

problems can be turned into catalysts to propel your business – your purpose – forward.

The biblical verse above also tells us that Jesus was proactively fulfilling a piece of the plan: "He who has shared my bread has turned against me." He reminds us that we need a plan and we need to refer back to the plan in order to stay aligned to our purpose, if we are going to bring about significant impact.

A true leader does not accept the status quo. He/she has the courage to share a vision of the future, as Jesus did. He/she has unique insight into the underpinnings and innerworkings of the business at hand. He/she is not simply reactive. And even in the face of adversity and betrayal, the next-level leader embraces the silver lining in the problem and has a steady confidence to predict proactively that it can all be used for good.

Jesus was able to be proactive because He did not allow fear to define Him, stop Him or slow Him down. He must have shocked the other disciples, but He was making a point. He was demonstrating visionary leadership – leading with a vision of the future, while connected to the past. He also showed that a leader cannot allow fear to rule. Fear makes you reactionary. Faith makes you move forward proactively without the need of others to tell you or approve of you.

Lord, make me more proactive to address the problems I see and can help solve. Remove the fear of man from me, so I can be boldly proactive and overcome any challenge.

MEDITATION: How have you been proactive in your life to address problems? What problem today could you be more proactive about?

SIXTEEN

END IN MIND

"Then Moses summoned Joshua and said to him in the presence of all Israel, 'Be strong and courageous, for you must go with this people into the land that the Lord swore to their ancestors to give them, and you must divide it among them as their inheritance. The Lord himself goes before you and will be with you; he will never leave you nor forsake you.'" (Deuteronomy 31:7-8)

Moses believed that God would lead Joshua and the Israelites into the Promised Land. They believed that their God had an end in mind for them, and they shared in the vision of "the land that the Lord swore to their ancestors to give them." Moses did not cross over the Jordan into this, let's say, "end-in-mind land," but Joshua was the one who went on to lead the Israelites into the Promised Land.

When you have an end in mind, the vision of it guides your next steps forward. However, if you have no ultimate goal in your business or in your personal life, then you are likely just wandering. In a sense, you are not going anywhere, even though you may always be moving and always staying busy. You are not aware of your "promised land."

Jorge L. Valdés, Ph.D. *in Collaboration with Anthony Petrucci*

When you are running a business, you want to envision what your "promised land" is. It may be a certain size company or hitting a certain revenue figure or buying a building to be your new offices or building an amazing product that customers want. It may be capturing a certain percentage of the market your company competes in. You have an end in mind. And once you reach it, you possess it and fully occupy it.

One other thing we can learn from this story of Moses and Joshua with the Promised Land is that you need to cross over something that may have its risks, its challenges and its setbacks. You may need to make tough business decisions before crossing over to your promised land. You may need to endure criticism before you can cross over. You may need to manage the uncertainty and ambiguity as you cross over. But because you know where you are headed, and you have declared it yours by faith – the end in mind – then you will find yourself being "strong and courageous."

And sometimes a leader, like Moses, takes the "company" only so far, and then another leader, like Joshua, needs to be risen up to take the company the "last mile" to the promised land. You may be Moses-like and are called to take a business or organization to a certain point, and then you will hand it off to another leader who has been prepared and will be ready for the "cross over." Just remember that it's not about you. It's about the people you are leading.

Lord, help me to keep the end in mind and not to get distracted by unimportant things that try to take my eyes off the promised land, which

Jorge L. Valdés, Ph.D. *in Collaboration with Anthony Petrucci*

You have laid out for me and the people I am leading (including children) and influencing.

MEDITATION: In the long term, what is the "end in mind" that drives you to do what you do or what inspires you to want to make changes, so you can reach this "end"? Are you seeking to provide for the financial security of your family? Are you trying to build a business that will propel others into prosperity? Do you want to guide the education and character development of your children? What is your "promised land" that will be a blessing?

Jorge L. Valdés, Ph.D. *in Collaboration with Anthony Petrucci*

SEVENTEEN

FIRST THING FIRST

"But since we belong to the day, let us be sober, putting on faith and love as a breastplate, and the hope of salvation as a helmet."

(1 Thessalonians 5:8)

The scriptures use a metaphor of "armor" to describe how to prepare to go out into the world and engage with people, things and situations. Clearly, it does not mean armor literally; it is intended to simplify the concepts for everyone. Before you do anything, you should get your mindset right (helmet of salvation) and your heart in the right place (breastplate of faith and love). Mindset and heart attitude are vital for affecting your outcome in almost anything in life. First thing first, indeed.

If your mindset is off, wrong, unstable or fluttering, then your impact will be much less or non-existent. If your heart attitude is full of resentment, anger, revenge, unforgiveness, despair and fear, then you will cast all of those things onto other people and you will become a burden to them. This usually happens when a person does not pay attention to their mindset or their heart attitude.

Jorge L. Valdés, Ph.D. *in Collaboration with Anthony Petrucci*

Wisdom from the Bible says to be deliberate about putting on the right mindset and to get a positive attitude, rooted in faith, hope and love, solidified within yourself. Then you will be ready to handle difficult people and difficult situations without being thrown off or crushed by any of them.

I recommend the "narco mindset" because it entails persevering through adversity, being a person of your word (integrity), thinking big, honoring others, paying attention to details, being committed to excellence, protecting your family, friends and business partners, avoiding any use of drugs completely (yes, the best narcos do not consume the drugs they sell; as only foolish people do drugs) and eschewing sloppiness and laziness.

You can definitely apply the narco mindset in lawful and honorable ways. (As I explain in my book *Narco Mindset*, if you apply the narco mindset to illicit activities, such as drug dealing, you will end up in jail or dead. Guaranteed.) You can put on the narco mindset, as if you are putting on a helmet. It will help protect you.

Furthermore, choosing to build your life on love and faith will benefit you. You access the law of planting and reaping, as you will reap what you sow. If you plant love into other people and speak faith, then love and faith will come back to you to bless you. If you plan hate, fear and faithlessness, you will receive the same in return. You can

Jorge L. Valdés, Ph.D. *in Collaboration with Anthony Petrucci*

protect your heart from being destroyed or compromised by covering yourself with love and faith.

Lord, guide me to put the most important things in life first – faith, hope and love. Protect my mind and my heart from negative thoughts and negative feelings. May I put on a mindset of excellence and a heart attitude of love modelled after You.

MEDITATION: Ponder the Great Commandment: "Love God with all your heart, your soul and your mind, and love your neighbor as yourself."

EIGHTEEN

WIN / WIN

"When pride comes, then comes disgrace, but with humility comes wisdom." (Proverbs 11:2)

A key to effective negotiation is to craft a win/win situation for both you and the one with whom you are negotiating. The best approach to do it is to humble yourself and put aside a self-centered, win/lose approach. So often, people think that there needs to be a "winner" and a "loser" in a negotiation. However, that is not true.

As the Scriptures tell us, humility brings wisdom, and one of the wisest things you can do is to consider what the other person wants and try to give them some of what they want in exchange for what you want. In this way, both you and the other side benefits, and the other person departs the negotiation feeling good, instead of resenting you. You are showing respect and that you are trying to understand what is really important to the other person.

If you only think of yourself, then you are exercising pride, instead of humility. With pride comes the other side's resentment, resistance and resolve. The other person may even be willing to give you more

Jorge L. Valdés, Ph.D. *in Collaboration with Anthony Petrucci*

than you think but because you are being stubbornly self-centered and refusing to work collaboratively on a win/win situation, he/she is going to make things harder for you. Even if you "win," the other person will come away feeling bad, used and discounted. In general, people don't like a braggart or "me first" winner. You will end up disgraced, either because the other person tells people how difficult you are or because stronger forces will form against you in a future negotiation to make sure you lose.

Yet, when you embrace humility and see the other person with respect, empathy and dignity, then you proactively seek out a win/win situation. In doing so, you exercise wisdom, resulting in greater blessings, which may not always be material possessions or money; they can also be a sense of peace and satisfaction, joy, compassion or a better reputation. People can trust you because you respect their best interests. Trust is very valuable in a world where people have difficulty finding anyone to truly trust. And when the Creator of the universe sees that he can trust you, then you gain His wisdom, and the sky's limit on how big of an impact you can make. With humility comes honor.

Lord, I choose to humble myself before you and I ask You to give me wisdom for how to deal with people in negotiations. I ask You to empower me with a keen ability to see win/win situations every time I negotiate anything, big or small.

MEDITATION: Think of a time when you "won" a negotiation in the short term, but, in the long run, lost because you hurt a relationship,

Jorge L. Valdés, Ph.D. *in Collaboration with Anthony Petrucci*

ruined your reputation, destroyed trust or demonstrated self-centeredness that turned off others. If you had chosen to be humble, how could you have turned that negotiation into a win/win in retrospect?

NINETEEN
UNDERSTAND BEFORE UNDERSTOOD

"When the turn came for Esther to go to the king, she asked for nothing other than what Hegai, the king's eunuch who was in charge of the harem, suggested. And Esther won the favor of everyone who saw her… Now the king was attracted to Esther more than to any of the other women, and she won his favor and approval more than any of the other [women]." (Esther 2:15-17)

Esther won favor with the king and became queen, and, as history shows, she would go on to save the Jewish people from destruction. However, if she had sought to be understood before "understanding," then she would have never become queen and, as a result, many Jewish people would have died. She could have demanded to be "understood" – namely, understood about how she was Jewish herself, how she was adopted by Mordecai and how she had faith in the God of Abraham, Isaac and Jacob. She could have also refused to do all the treatments that the eunuch suggested because she only wanted things her way.

Jorge L. Valdés, Ph.D. *in Collaboration with Anthony Petrucci*

In the business world, Esther's approach equates to a salesperson or marketing professional seeking to understand the customer. Rather than pushing product details down a customer's throat to be understood, you proactively seek to understand the customer's needs and pain points, making preparations to be at your best to meet the customer's expectations and win a bigger contract.

First, Esther took Mordacai's advice and did not reveal her true nationality. It would have been a distraction or a nail in the proverbial coffin of any chance to become queen. It would have also likely triggered attempts to kill her. What we learn from her here that can be applied to a business is that, even as a person of faith, you still need to be skillful in negotiation. What to reveal and what not to reveal too quickly are key to effective negotiations.

Second, Esther listened and sought to understand the protocol for getting ready to be presented to the king. She went through the beauty treatments and ate the special food that the eunuch suggested. She understood that there was a process to being her best. It was not going to happen overnight or by seeking self-gratification. She wasn't eating sugar cookies or greasy burgers every day. She was understanding what was required. Likewise, in business, we are smart to understand the process, the requirements and the recommended preparation.

Esther also sought to understand the king and what was important to him. God had put her in a unique situation, but she had to put aside her own agenda to glorify herself and stay flexible in understanding the

73

moment at hand. In the end, her understanding led her to put her people, the Jewish people, first, rather than demanding that she be "understood" like a diva would. With understanding, she fulfilled her purpose. In a business context, this is similar to putting the customer first.

Lord, help me to understand before being understood. It's not about me. It's about the higher purpose for which I live and take action. Help me to submit to the process that is required for You to promote me.

MEDITATION: Think of a time when you proactively sought out to understand someone else, listening to them and holding yourself back, so you put them first. How were you blessed by it?

Jorge L. Valdés, Ph.D. *in Collaboration with Anthony Petrucci*

TWENTY

SYNERGY

"My prayers for all of them is that they will be one, just as you and I are one, Father that just as you are in me and I am in you, so they will be in us, and the world will believe you sent me." (John 17: 21)

In his book, *The 7 Habits of Highly Effective People*, Stephen R. Covey posits that "synergy is the essence of principle-centered leadership.   It is the essence of principle-centered parenting.   It catalyzes, unifies, and unleashes the greatest powers within people." (pg. 262)

In essence, we know that an organization possesses synergy when the whole of that organization is greater than its individual parts. Why then is such an amazing concept so difficult to attain?   In today's workplace, the reason 70 percent of employees leave their jobs is because they do not feel appreciated. Combine this with all the energy spent by management in conflict resolution and one can appreciate how synergy in the workplace has the potential to impact our economy dramatically.   If people could work together for one common goal, placing others above self, we could reduce 70 percent of the turnover which cost companies billions of dollars.

Lack of synergy is not only relegated to the workforce. I suggest that lack of synergy between families is one of the major reasons for the chaos of the American family. It's a chaos that has become a core reason for such high drug and suicide problems among youth today. It seems that individualism has won over the ideal of placing the interest of others above self. In a world where adults are obsessed with satisfying the lust of their flesh, others become victims, especially the youth, most painfully.

As we read the prayer above, Jesus is not praying for people to become human drones but for a unity grounded in something greater than self - our Creator. The prayer is not for people to be carbon copies of each other but for people to find oneness - synergy with their Creator. And, as we do this, we then find oneness with each other; then synergy is best exemplified in an identity that seeks what is best for others as we value them as unique interventions of our Creator.

It is only when people see that we are able to find unity through our Creator, not only in our workplace but in our families, too, that the world then would want to exemplify this synergy. Synergy, in essence, is oneness, only achievable through our oneness with our Creator; we seek a higher power than ourselves. A power exemplified by a sacrificial death. No greater love exists than that when we die for others.

Lord, allow me to find oneness with you so that I can then find synergy with others.

MEDITATION: Think back: when was the last time you placed the interest of others above your own interests?

Jorge L. Valdés, Ph.D. *in Collaboration with Anthony Petrucci*

TWENTY-ONE
SHARPEN THE SAW

"I am the true vine, and my Father is the gardener. He cuts off every branch in me that bears no fruit, while every branch that does bear fruit he prunes so that it will be even more fruitful. You are already clean because of the word I have spoken to you. Remain in me, as I also remain in you. No branch can bear fruit by itself; it must remain in the vine. Neither can you bear fruit unless you remain in me." (John 15:1-4)

Using a metaphor about a gardener pruning the branches in a vineyard, Jesus revealed a key to success in one's life – spiritual, emotional and physical – as well success in one's business. Pruning means trimming to cut away dead or overgrown branches or stems. Jesus makes the point that the reason for cutting away is "so that it will be even more fruitful."

For a person or a business to grow, pruning, trimming, sharpening or whatever word you want to use to represent a cutting away is necessary to increase better outcomes and prevent the dead or overgrown things from choking the life out of your business or destroying your dreams and goals in life. You may need to sharpen your saw to cut off old mindsets that have held you back.

Jorge L. Valdés, Ph.D. *in Collaboration with Anthony Petrucci*

You may have had a mindset and a set of beliefs that produced little to no good in your life. You may feel like you are on a treadmill and living the same mundane, dissatisfying life every day over and over, as if it's Groundhog Day replaying itself day after day. You may think too small of yourself or have lost a sense of your true identity as a successful, forward-thinking adventurer with the capacity to improve the world. You may have fallen into a "dead" way of thinking that you don't have what it takes to be successful in life.

No, it is time for you to sharpen your saw and cut that self-defeating mindset and that false belief out of your mind and soul. You should do some pruning of your thinking, which you have power over, so you can make room for new, revitalizing mindsets that renew and grow you on a personal and professional level.

You should do some pruning with your sharpened saw of what you say and think about yourself, so you can allow your true identity as a person whom God loves and helps to emerge. Then, to use of Jesus' metaphor, you will bear fruit in your personal and professional life.

Lord, I ask You to help me prune the negative thought patterns, false beliefs and sense of shame that undermine my ability to be the best person You created me to be. Give me the courage to face the reality of my inner life so that I may cut out what needs to be eliminated.

Jorge L. Valdés, Ph.D. *in Collaboration with Anthony Petrucci*

MEDITATION: What conscious and subconscious attitudes, beliefs, emotions and thought patterns need to be trimmed back or removed out of myself?

Jorge L. Valdés, Ph.D. *in Collaboration with Anthony Petrucci*

SEVEN STRONG

CHARACTER

TRAITS

Jorge L. Valdés, Ph.D. *in Collaboration with Anthony Petrucci*

TWENTY-TWO
INTEGRITY

"A good name is to be chosen rather than great riches, and favor is better than silver or gold." (Proverbs 22:1)

The word "integrity" is one that has gone through a metamorphic change. As we look back through just a couple of generations before us and look at the way business was conducted during our grandparents' time, we can see the change in the meaning of the word. I remember clearly as a child in Cuba going to the grocery store and picking up things for dinner and telling the grocer that my grandmother had sent me; he would nod and make a note in what I consider some type an account book. There was no doubt in that grocer's mind that my family would pay that bill.

Coming to America and going through a very difficult time as a young immigrant child and often times going without food to eat, I will never forget the speech my dad would give my brother and me over and over again: "Son, you have no control in life of whether you are rich or poor; many things can influence this. Son, you have no control in life whether you are sick or healthy, nor whether you are dead or alive; son, the only thing you have absolute control of is your word; only you have the power to make your word mean something or not mean anything at all." This repeated lesson one day would propel me to lay in a Panamanian jail dying because of my refusal to give up the only thing I had absolute power of: my word.

The World War II generation was defined as a generation where a person's ethics defined their decisions. Today, in our morally relative world we have it backwards; today our decisions are what define our ethics; therefore, "integrity" is ethically relative. Where once our word was our bond, and the thought of breaking it would not even cross a person's mind, today a person's word is only as good as the contracts we have drawn up to enforce our word.

In a world where we do what is most convenient and we are constantly looking out for "what is in it for me," our word fluctuates with the weather. We assume that no one likes a liar, yet as we fail to do what we say we will do, we become adamant liars.

Integrity is best defined as what we do when no one else is looking. I suggest today that even though we think that no one is looking, in reality, He who created us is ever present. As business leaders and leaders of our families, we need to allow our word to define us as the people we are.

Lord, when I am in doubt, remind me that a good name based on keeping my word is more precious than all that can be acquired.

Jorge L. Valdés, Ph.D. *in Collaboration with Anthony Petrucci*

MEDITATION: As you lead your family and empower your children to be our nation's future leaders, is integrity a subject that is critically present or ever absent?

Jorge L. Valdés, Ph.D. *in Collaboration with Anthony Petrucci*

TWENTY-THREE
SERVANT

*"Then James and John, the sons of Zebedee, came over and spoke to him,
'Teacher,' they said, 'we want you to do us a favor.' 'What is it?' he asked.
In your glorious Kingdom, we want to sit in places of honor next to you' . . .
Jesus answered, 'You don't know what you are asking! . . . You know that in
this world kings are tyrants, and officials lord over the people beneath them.
But among you it should be quite different. Whoever wants to be a leader
among you must be your servant, and whoever wants to be first must be the
slave of all.'" (John 10: 35-38, 42-44).*

Since this passage was written, two thousand years have passed and
yet today we still strive for a position of authority where we can, instead
of leading people, rule over them. It seems that the old saying "look
out for number one" has, in fact, become a way of life.

The concept of being a "servant" is very misunderstood. Society
equates servanthood with slavery -- a position to be avoided at all cost.
It is very difficult for parents to teach their children that there is great
honor in serving someone. If we look around our business world,
seldom do we find a vendor whose mission is to be a servant to his
client. Often times we are left feeling as if they are doing us a great

Jorge L. Valdés, Ph.D. *in Collaboration with Anthony Petrucci*

favor by taking our money. Most often we strive to get the better hand of the deal, and our satisfaction lies not in that we give our customers 110% value for their money, but that we took them for all we could and got away with giving as little as we could get away with. After all, is this not in fact a way to control cost in a competitive economy?

The same principle dominates our workplace. For many titles are more important than economic remuneration. I knew many who were happier with a business card with a big title than a paycheck. Among different levels of management, the mission is not what is best for our company and, thus, for our customers, but in "what is in it for me?" We seem to focus on the "now" instead of the "tomorrow"; on us, instead of them.

I am often asked how my wife and I began a small company with a $500 investment in the basement of our home and grew it to a million-dollar thriving company in less than four years? We do not have to hesitate. We simply decided that we were going to do what others had a problem doing. We would honor God in all we did by serving our customers; we would give our customers more than what they paid for. Simple, yet so seemingly difficult to implement in today's cut-throat business world.

The concept of being a servant was extremely difficult for Jesus' followers to grasp, too. After all, how can He, whom they believed to be God, wash their feet? Was this act not restricted to the lowest of slaves? Yet, it would be the foundation of the Christian faith. Their

Messiah was not coming like King David in a warrior's horse to win some type of political war and liberate them from the Romans. He was coming sitting on a donkey to die for them and expect them to die for others. So revolutionary was the thought that many who followed him left him. Yet, this revolutionary act would change the course of humanity.

It is only in the act of serving others that true freedom lies. It is in the act of giving of us to others that true victories are won. It changed the Roman-Greco world and it can change our business world today. I suggest that if we teach our children as well as our fellow employees to ask not what others can do for them, but what they can do for others, as we place the welfare of others above ours, we can, in fact, change our business world and our families.

Lord, allow me today to place the interest of others above mine. Allow me to serve others.

MEDITATION: How important are others above you? How important is the welfare of your children and spouse above yours?

TWENTY-FOUR

VISION

"Where there is no vision, the people perish but he that keeps the law happy is he." (Proverbs 29:16).

"I see a union and a confederation of thirteen states, independent of Parliament, of Minister and of King!" (John Adams, 1774). In his book *The Founding Fathers of Leadership*, Donald T. Phillips posits that before a creative leader attempts to inspire others, he must have a good idea of where he wants to go. "As such, a vision is at the heart of leadership."

Such was the case with John Adams. We often believe that to be a great leader one must have an amazing education, preferably from a prestigious university, but this was not the case with John Adams, who was born and raised in very humble surroundings. Adam's father worked as a farmer and a shoemaker, and his mother instilled in him a strong Christian upbringing. He spent a considerable part of his life reading and learning. He decided never to "suffer one hour to pass unimproved."

John Adams was driven to succeed. At times he felt that he was destined for greatness and other times he was extremely humble. When elected to Congress, he believed that a new opportunity had arisen for him, yet he felt himself "unequal" to the task (according to his diary). In May of 1774 the Virginia House of Burgess called for a gathering of representatives from all colonies. From this gathering surfaced the First Continental Congress on September 5, 1774. Immediately, there was division among the delegates, especially between the radicals, who were determined to change the relationship with Great Britain, and the conservatives, who had commercial ties to Great Britain and advocated diplomacy.

The opportunities to lead aroused, and Adams seized the moment. He led the radicals with finesse and delicateness. Adams began to whisper to all delegates the word "independence." As everyone thought about it, they could understand it. "Soon it was on the lips of many representatives until it became their own idea - not just that of John Adams."

Great leaders do not impose their thoughts on others. They lead by example, as they empower others to appropriate leadership and innovation. Anyone can impose fear on another person, but respect is earned. Many so-called business leaders have no knowledge of empowerment because they lack foundational principles. Therefore, they dictate to those who most follow; as a result, we find many companies perishing daily. They perish because of no vision. And the circle is never ending.

Jorge L. Valdés, Ph.D. *in Collaboration with Anthony Petrucci*

Many suggest that John Adams knew how to communicate his vision clearly as a direct result of being "a scholar of the Scriptures." (Phillips, 34)

Lord, give me a hunger for your Scriptures so that in them I can find the wisdom to lead those with whom you have blessed me.

MEDITATION: Is there any correlation between leadership and the Scriptures?

Jorge L. Valdés, Ph.D. *in Collaboration with Anthony Petrucci*

TWENTY-FIVE
TEAM PLAYER

"Paul decided to go to Jerusalem, passing through Macedonia and Achaia. 'After I have been there,' he said, 'I must visit Rome also.' He sent two of his helpers, Timothy and Erastus, to Macedonia, while he stayed in the province of Asia a little longer." (Acts 19:21-22)

Every leader and every organization need team players. A team player puts his/her own self-centered interests aside to take on the vision, objectives and purpose of the organization or the visionary leader. In the New Testament, Paul had a "helper" named Timothy, who supported and co-labored with Paul.

Not everyone can be the big star or the focus point of an organization. Team players consistently do what many may consider routine work. They go places where the top leader cannot be at any given time, but all the while representing the leader and the purpose of the organization. They do what is needed for the greater good, even if it's inconvenient or difficult for them. They work hard to stay aligned to the purpose of the leader or the organization. There is power in alignment.

91

A business leader cannot be in two places at the same time – although technology sometimes makes us believe we can be in multiple meetings at the same time, thanks to videoconferencing, mobile phones, skype and Facetime. A team player makes sure to deliver the same consistent messages that the leader would, if the leader was in the place where the team player is. An organization replicates itself, amplifies itself and propagates itself through committed team players.

Every manager knows the old saying, "Good help is hard to find." It is not automatic that an employee will be a team player. Most tend not to be, at least not genuinely. But when you find a true team player, you need to cultivate them, nurture them, encourage them and train them. A person can have a great attitude as a team player, but not have the knowledge, skills or know-how to be effective. Therefore, it is important to train and equip team players, so they will be at their best, representing you and your organization.

And if you are an employee, you may face the decision whether to be a team player or not. Sure, you can go through the motions, but when you are sincere, it shows. If you want your boss to value your contributions to the company to a great measure, become a team player. Get aligned with the higher-level objectives and purpose. Find out what is important to your manager and be there when they need you. As a result, you will be honored.

Jorge L. Valdés, Ph.D. *in Collaboration with Anthony Petrucci*

Lord, give me a heart to be a team player, with the most important role I have under your leadership to show the world the power of a transformed life – my life, thanks to you.

MEDITATION: What does being a team player mean to you? How have you been a team player? How are some of the best team players you have ever known in your career?

Jorge L. Valdés, Ph.D. *in Collaboration with Anthony Petrucci*

TWENTY-SIX

LIKEABLE

"Many seek the rulers favor, but justice comes from the Lord."

(Proverbs 29:26)

As we ponder over the nature of our morals, ethicists suggest that morality is only a by-product of religion or culture. For this devotional I want to focus on culture and its influence not only on our morals, but also on the choices we make on a daily basis.

It is often suggested that what defined the World War II generation, which came to be known as the "Greatest Generation," was that their decisions were based on their ethics. Today, it seems that it is the reverse; our ethics are based mostly on those decisions we make daily in our workplace. Most of the time our decisions are driven by our desire to be "likeable" in our constant search for the approval of those around us.

As we constantly seek the approval of our parents, teachers and our peers in the workplace, we find that most of the time, no matter what we do, it is never enough. We spend countless hours in the gym seeking

Jorge L. Valdés, Ph.D. *in Collaboration with Anthony Petrucci*

the approval of those of the opposite gender; we take all kind of classes to better ourselves and perhaps get that promotion we so deserve; and somehow it seems that time and time again we find ourselves coming short. Yet, we never consider that God rarely uses those whose drive is based on what others think of themselves.

In his book *The Traveler's Gift*, Andrew Stanley presents a series of conversation sbetween David, the main character in the book, who suddenly encounters himself being taught by amazing historical figures. In one conversation with President Abraham Lincoln, David asks the President, "Are you bothered by what other people are saying about you?" Lincoln responds, "As you may know, I am the first ever Republican president. I was elected by a minority of the popular vote, and even some members of my own cabinet view me as third-rate. To many of the elite of Washington, I will always be a country lawyer, a gawky, unrefined outsider. If I were to concern myself with the newspaper columns that label me dishonest and stupid, if I had my feelings destroyed every time a political opponent called me an ape or a buffoon, I would never be about the work for which I was born. . . . Sooner or later every man of character will have that character questioned. Every man of honor will be faced with unjust criticism, but never forget that unjust criticism has no impact whatsoever upon the truth. And the only sure way to avoid criticism is to do nothing and be nothing!"

Lincoln would go on to sign one of the most important documents humanity would ever know: the Emancipation Proclamation, which would reaffirm God's intention that every man, woman and child was created equal. This document brought enormous harsh criticism, however, for Lincoln; public opinion may sway like a tide, but right and wrong will not. I wonder where our nation and the world would be if this man of God was more concerned with public opinion than with doing the work for which he knew he was born.

Our goal in life is not to seek the public's approval in all we do, but to accomplish that for which we were created. How then are we to know what we were created for if we did not create ourselves? Only a Creator knows for sure for what purpose he created something.

Lord, give me a hunger for your manual for creation. Allow me to seek your approval and not that of others.

MEDITATION: Are you certain you know what you were created for?

Jorge L. Valdés, Ph.D. *in Collaboration with Anthony Petrucci*

TWENTY-SEVEN

FORGIVENESS

"Now it is time to forgive him and comfort him. Otherwise he may become so discouraged that he won't be able to recover. Now show him that you still love him." (2 Corinthians 2: 7-8)

When we think about forgiveness, we have a mindset of someone who has done wrong coming to us and asking us to forgive him; this act in itself places us on a "one up" position over that person. Yet, the real power that the forgiveness provides lies not in us forgiving those who ask us to forgive them but in us forgiving those who do not ask and, more importantly, are really hard to forgive.

As we travel through this hard road called life, most of us can quickly recollect many instances where people have hurt us and never repented. Some of those acts hurt us so much that we hold them inside and often allow them to consume our entire life. We cannot conceive that someone can do us wrong and not ask us to forgive them. It pains us. It angers us, and it lives in our heart for what seems eternity. We contemplate revenge and slowly it ends us being expressed in the many wrong choices we make.

Jorge L. Valdés, Ph.D. *in Collaboration with Anthony Petrucci*

One vivid memory, which I cannot forget, involves my family. When I was in my early twenties, my father was unfaithful to my mom. She found out and I thought our family would crumble. My mom, being the strong woman that she was, determined that she would never divorce my father and break up her family; however, she would never forgive him for it. In my father's last hours, he called my brother, my mom and me into the room where he was laying and prayed that God would forgive him for all his sins, as he thanked God for the all he had given him. He turned to my mom and asked her to forgive him; she looked at him and walked out of the room. This act destroyed my brother and me, and it ended up consuming her life.

It is only when we pray for a spirit of forgiveness that we can forgive those who have hurt us and do not seem to care or repent that we are liberated from the forces that cause turmoil for us, as we toil with the many thoughts that follow. When we pray for those who have hurt us, we become Christ-like; then, just as Christ prayed that God would forgive them, for they did not know what they were doing, we are liberated by the greatest expression of love: loving those who are not loveable, even at their most unlovable moments. "Father, forgive these people, because they don't know what they are doing." (Luke 23: 34)

Lord, allow me to love those who hurt me and give me the strength to find a spirit of forgiveness, even when they do not show any remorse.

MEDITATION: Can you think of a time when someone has hurt you and the pain still hunts you today? If you can, stop right now and forgive them. Remember the old adage: forgiveness is divine.

Jorge L. Valdés, Ph.D. *in Collaboration with Anthony Petrucci*

TWENTY-EIGHT
COMPASSIONATE

"But when He saw the multitudes, He was moved with compassion on them, because they fainted, and were scattered abroad as sheep having no Shepard." (Matthew 9:36)

Often when we look back on our lives, we wonder why it is that we have not made a difference in anyone else's life. We worked hard; we sacrificed much, and often success was the by-product of our hard work. But the question then becomes: how do we measure success? Is success measured by assets, or by an income statement? If it is, then success is limited to time and place. Then, if the economy suddenly takes a turn for the worst and we find ourselves financially destitute, are we then not successful?

As I look back on my life, I remember pondering over my father who went from being a very rich man in our country of Cuba to losing it all and working at a Jackson Byron store as a janitor. The fact that my father never complained about what I thought were "bum cards" that life had given him, often times irritating me, and even at the age of 10 years old, I wondered if my father was a failure. It would take many

Jorge L. Valdés, Ph.D. *in Collaboration with Anthony Petrucci*

years for me to realize that my father was a giant and that his success was not measured by dollars.

My father was a giant of a man not only because he faced his economic hardships with an amazing amount of dignity, but because he was also a compassionate man. He gave a hand to anyone whom he thought was less fortunate than us, often sacrificing food at our dinner table. He had compassion on all who knocked at our door. When he was not repaid for money, he would still give, he never complained. Many times my mother would be angry that people were stealing from him, but to him they were not. He would say: "How could they steal from me when I do not expect them to pay me back?"

It is hard to live up to my father's example. It is my desire that, if my children ever remember me for anything, it will be for the fact that I have compassion for others. People are not a commodity to be exploited for a certain amount of time in the workplace. They are God's creation for us to show the same compassion that Christ has shown us, when He paid the ultimate sacrifice.

Lord, strengthen me to be compassionate to all who are scattered like a sheep without a Sheppard.

MEDITATION: Take a moment of solitude and ask yourself," When the last time you showed compassion to others?"

TWENTY-NINE

GOSSIP

"A gossip betrays a confidence, but a trustworthy person keeps a secret."
(Proverbs 11:13)

In today's society, more people seem more interested in juicy gossip than they are interested in truth, trust or respect for others. Tabloids are still popular at supermarkets because people want to consume "dirt" about celebrities. Co-workers in a company gossip about each other to try to get an edge, demean others for their own benefit, and appear as a source of salacious tidbits that seemingly lift people out of the humdrum of mundane daily life. Even people at churches spread gossip about other churchgoers, turning prayer requests into fuel for gossip.

But the Bible clear states that gossiping is dangerous, damaging and downright wrong. It is a timeless principle that, if a person gossips about another person after finding out something private or confidential about the person at hand, the action to gossip has consequences: it destroys trust, ruins relationships and sparks anger and resentment.

Jorge L. Valdés, Ph.D. *in Collaboration with Anthony Petrucci*

So how is it that something so potentially damaging and flammable as gossip is built into the core foundation of today's culture so nonchalantly and approvingly, as if gossip is America's favorite pastime? Has society lost its mind to encourage and validate gossip? Does anyone care about the consequences of gossip in people's lives? What does the chronic gossiping say about today's culture, the character of the average adult and human nature itself?

It has gotten to the point at which if you do not gossip, you seem "strange" and do not "fit in" with the crowd. You can actually make people uncomfortable by refusing to participate in gossip.

We live in a world of decreasing trust. People don't trust each other anymore, for the most part. With gossip so rampant, is there any wonder? So when a person chooses to respect another person and keep the other person's secret or confidential piece of information, it breeds and increases trust. To be considered a trustworthy person, you need to be consistent, which means making it a habit NOT to gossip. When you keep a secret, you are covering the other person with respect and love. You are not aiming to hurt their reputation or credibility.

Then when other people see that you have a track record of keeping secrets and honoring others by your discretion, they will trust you and tell you more confidential information in order to be transparent. So many people are yearning to be transparent, but they don't know who they can be transparent with. You may not be able to be everyone's confidante, but you can start today to be someone's trustworthy friend by refusing to spread gossip about them. Be different.

Lord, please show me when I make the mistake of speaking gossip about another person; help me to admit my mistake quickly and promptly make amends. Help me to be a consistently trustworthy person.

MEDITATION: How have you liked it in the past when someone gossiped about you? Have you gossiped about anyone? How can you make amends about it?

Jorge L. Valdés, Ph.D. *in Collaboration with Anthony Petrucci*

THIRTY

CHEATING

"The LORD said to Moses: 'If anyone sins and is unfaithful to the LORD by deceiving a neighbor about something entrusted to them or left in their care or about something stolen, or if they cheat their neighbor, ... They must make restitution in full...'" (Leviticus 6:1-2, 5)

If your parent considers cheating to be morally wrong and you go cheat someone out of something, you are not only violating a rule set down by a higher authority, but you are hurting your parent, disrespecting your parent and declaring yourself as your own moral authority. In the scripture verse above, it's interesting that Moses wrote that cheating is wrong (a "sin"), not simply because someone arbitrarily laid down a law, but it is also considered an act of unfaithfulness to the Lord God Himself.

What that essentially means is that cheating does not fit your true identity as what a human being was intended to be. The act of cheating is a lowering of a person's dignity and it goes against the core values of giving to others, helping others and being unselfish. Cheating is an act of selfishness and pride wrapped up in entitlement.

Jorge L. Valdés, Ph.D. *in Collaboration with Anthony Petrucci*

When someone cheats at work by reporting inflated numbers to look better or getting sensitive information unfairly to take more of their fair share, it reveals selfishness and, like gossip, destroys trust. In today's world, some would argue that cheating is okay as long as you don't get caught.

First of all, the Creator of the universe sees the cheating. Second, you know what cheating is, so it searches the human conscience. Third, cheating always comes back to bite a person one way or another. As a cheater, a person will not be given more responsibility. In a way, cheating cheats a person out of having the best in life – God's best in life.

Extramarital affairs are also a form of cheating. Surveys reveal that a high number of married people cheat on their spouses, and many don't feel bad about it or think it is wrong. In fact, one of the world's top relationship experts is now saying that extramarital affairs (infidelity) can "result in good things." But this moral relativism clearly shows that the lowly mindset to endorse infidelity is simply trying to adapt to today's culture, not taking into account timeless principles, emotional realities or spiritual laws. Rather than saying "cheating on your spouse is wrong or immoral," the message is "cheat if it makes you feel better." This is the "me first" mantra on steroids.

Have we come to a point as a society that cheating is the standard, while excellence in a married relationship is non-existent because a whole generation has lost sight of what "excellence" even means for a relationship?

Lord, help me to always see cheating of any kind the way you see it, as an act of unfaithfulness toward you and as a compromise that cheats me out of receiving your best for my life.

MEDITATION: Have you ever cheated someone out of something of value? Is there an opportunity for you to make amends with the person, even if years later?

Jorge L. Valdés, Ph.D. *in Collaboration with Anthony Petrucci*

THIRTY-ONE

LYING

"There are six things the Lord hates - no, seven things he detests: haughty eyes, a lying tongue, hands that kill the innocent, a heart that plots evil, feet that race to wrong, a false witness who pours out lies, a person who sows discord among brothers." (Proverbs 6: 16-19)

TIME magazine would label the summer of 2002 as the "Summer of Mistrust" and would report that "Most Americans − 72% in the Time/CNN poll − fear that they were not a few isolated cases but a pattern of deception by a large number of companies (Nancy Gibbs, "Summer of Mistrust," Time, July 22, 2002).

The fall of Enron would cost investors over 60 billions dollars, wipe out millions of American's retirement, and be the beginning of many more tragic stories, such as Adelphia, WorldCom, and many other bankruptcies. George Barna asked Americans at the time if they had complete confidence that leaders in various professions would consistently make morally appropriate decisions in their workplace. ("Americans Speak: Enron, WorldCom and Others Are Results of Inadequate Moral Training by Families," July 2002, Barna Research Online), The answer was very sad.

Jorge L. Valdés, Ph.D. *in Collaboration with Anthony Petrucci*

The research inquired about leaders who were executives of large corporations, elected government officials, film producers, directors and writers, small business owners, ministers and teachers. Of the above, teachers received by far the highest vote of confidence, 14 percent of all teachers hold the public's complete confidence. Yet, it is sad that even though teachers are held as the most trusted leaders, 6 out of 7 Americans are not willing to trust them. Where does this mistrust begin?

From the above research we deduce that lying is not secluded to the almighty corporate America. It is something that permeates every level of our society from small business owners, to ministers, to politicians to teachers. I suggest that our moral decay has been a process fueled by postmodern thought. It began when we allowed our culture to suggest that there was no absolute truth; all truths are valid, and there was no final authority to define right and wrong.

Right and wrong is secluded to what a particular culture decides is right and wrong, they say. The absence of absolute truth creates a vacuum where to find definitive answers.

If we look at the above Scripture, we find that God detests a lie. When our society feared God, a handshake was sufficient for people to reach agreements. We placed great trust in God-fearing leaders who would create the nation we proudly call America. We did not separate our faith from our workplace, and, in essence, our success was attributed to our faith. If God's Word is not authoritative and all goes, then no longer can we do business on a handshake; we need one contract to finalize a transaction and another to protect the original contract.

Lord, help me to fear God and hear His admonitions.

MEDITATION: Is our motivation to tell the truth based on the fact that God has defined a lie as a detestable practice?

Jorge L. Valdés, Ph.D. *in Collaboration with Anthony Petrucci*

THIRTY-TWO

SELFISH

"Then one of the Twelve—the one called Judas Iscariot—went to the chief priests and asked, 'What are you willing to give me if I deliver him over to you?' So they counted out for him thirty pieces of silver. From then on Judas watched for an opportunity to hand him over." (Matthew 26:14-16)

Judas Iscariot was selfishly seeking money in exchange for handing over Jesus Christ to the chief priests. He did not consider or understand the consequences of his selfish act. He was simply enticed by the prospect of getting money for his own selfish desires. You may say that what Judas exhibited was "greed." While this is also true, the root of it is selfishness.

I bring this up because we live in a world where society exalts money and material things, so people chase these temporal things selfishly – not caring or counting the cost of how it will affect their children, spouse, family, friends or colleagues at work.

When a co-worker steps on others, undermines colleagues and does whatever it takes to selfishly get ahead in order to get the promotion and the big raise in salary, selfishness is embedded in everything the person does. The person wants the money as well as the personal glory. Therefore, this same person will not make the best decisions for the team, will not consider how decisions will impact other people and will not selflessly sacrifice for the good of the company or the team when the time comes for an employee or a leader to do the honorable thing. Selfishness has skewed the ability to see clearly or soberly. As a result, organizations, families and relationships suffer accordingly.

Being selfish makes a person not think twice about betraying another person. Some would say, "It's a dog eat dog world." Or "you have to look out for number one." But it doesn't have to be that way. It is that way because people have decided that exalting selfishness is easier and better for instant gratification. Yet, when a person delays gratification and opens up his or her heart to consider other people, then selfish decisions give way to unselfish decisions, and suddenly, the world becomes a little better of a place where someone chose NOT to act selfishly, even though the temptation still lingered.

Does history judge Judas Iscariot in a positive light for his selfish act of betrayal? No, not at all. Because of his selfishness that turned into greed, his name is forever associated with "betrayal." Judas put himself first and then, in the end, he was made last. When one chooses to put himself last, then, in the end, he is made first. It's a spiritual principle that is operating in the world today, but so few people know about it.

Jorge L. Valdés, Ph.D. *in Collaboration with Anthony Petrucci*

Selfishness can turn into lust that turns into sex outside marriage. Selfishness can turn into hate that turns into hurting or killing another person. Selfishness can turn into revenge that turns into destroying a co-worker's reputation in order to get ahead of that person. Selfishness can turn into jealousy that turns into a refusal to collaborate openly and effectively with a co-worker, thus hurting the company.

What corporate America does not realize is that selfishness is killing it and the people who work in it. A change is needed, and companies would do themselves a favor to reward unselfish behavior and promptly expose selfish behavior.

Lord, I ask you to reveal to me the hidden selfishness within me, and help me to choose to be unselfish, even when it would be easy and convenient for me to be selfish.

MEDITATION: How have you been selfish in the past? How have you been unselfish in the past? Did any certain unselfish acts have negative short-term consequences, but you can now see positive long-term effects of your unselfish act?

THIRTY-THREE
ARROGANT

"...as the king was walking on the roof of the royal palace of Babylon, he said, 'Is not this the great Babylon I have built as the royal residence, by my mighty power and for the glory of my majesty?' Even as the words were on his lips, a voice came from heaven, 'This is what is decreed for you, King Nebuchadnezzar: Your royal authority has been taken from you...'. Now I, Nebuchadnezzar, praise and exalt and glorify the King of heaven, because everything he does is right and all his ways are just. And those who walk in pride he is able to humble." (Daniel 4:29-31, 37)

King Nebuchadnezzar of Babylon learned that the biblical revelation about arrogance – "Pride comes before a fall" – is true. Just as the king was thinking arrogant thoughts and glorifying himself for his accomplishment, the Lord responded by humbling him. It is part of a spiritual law on earth: humble yourself and the Lord will raise you up; raise yourself up and the Lord will humble you. Just ask King Nebuchadnezzar how true this is.

Arrogance is ugly, deceptive, isolating, destructive and something that evidently does not sit well with the Creator of the universe. People don't warm up to arrogant people, in general. Arrogance creates a separation between people. It makes the person believe he/she is so special that he/she is above everyone else, even though it is not true because God created everyone equal. Arrogance leads a person to be condescending to others, to have a "diva" attitude, to have a sense of entitlement and to think of himself/herself as God, with power, prestige and/or wealth or simply something that seems superior.

Arrogance blinds a person to reality. In the business world, an arrogant business leader may assume that the competition can never catch up with his company's market share leadership because the company is so dominant; however, the next thing he knows is that a competitor has surpassed his company in market share. He had been so arrogant that he did not put customers first, did not stay committed to continuous improvement and did not treat his employees well. Arrogance had led him to become complacent, which is a dangerous thing in business.

When reality shows you that you need to change, arrogance tells you to stay the same: "you're the best after all." When reality shows you to learn new things from your customers, arrogance tells you that you know all there is to know about your customers: "you're the best after all." When reality shows you reduce spending before you get into financial trouble, arrogance tells you to keep spending because money will keep rolling in: "you're the best after all." When you humble yourself in business and commit to continuous improvement, you put yourself in a better position to not believe the lies that arrogance tells everyone.

Lord, give me a new revelation of my own arrogance. Where do I need to change by first humbling myself? How can I get better?

MEDITATION: Can you think of a time when you were so arrogant about something, such as winning a game or being first, that you ended up losing? How did arrogance prevent you from giving your best?

Jorge L. Valdés, Ph.D. *in Collaboration with Anthony Petrucci*

THIRTY-FOUR
MERCILESS

"When Herod realized that he had been outwitted by the Magi, he was furious, and he gave orders to kill all the boys in Bethlehem and its vicinity who were two years old and under, in accordance with the time he had learned from the Magi." (Matthew 2:16)

Because King Herod feared and hated that Jesus Christ was considered the Messiah, he ordered all the boys under the age of two to be killed in Bethlehem and in the surrounding areas. He was merciless in his murderous desires. He did not care at all that the mothers and fathers of all those other children would suffer because their children, who were innocent, would be killed by a king without mercy.

So many people think that God is without mercy because he allows people to get sick and die; he allows wars and violence to take place in this world on a regular basis; and he seems silent or elsewhere when many people need help or even a miracle. However, the Bible tells us over and over that God is a God of mercy. It is Satan who is without mercy and selfish. And when a man's heart is hardened by sin or by blind self-centeredness, he can become merciless.

Jorge L. Valdés, Ph.D. *in Collaboration with Anthony Petrucci*

To have mercy on someone is to pull back from hurting them because you love your neighbor as yourself. You would not want a more powerful person to harm you, so you don't do it to someone else. If a higher authority than King Herod had decreed that King Herod should be captured, tortured and killed, Herod would likely beg for mercy. It is hypocrisy to be merciless toward others but expect mercy for oneself. The law remains: you reap what you sow.

When a business leader responds to an employee, who has made a mistake, by showing mercy and taking the stance that the employee has learned something valuable through the mistake, the leader will gain the loyalty of the employee for the long term. When an employee expects a business leader to come down on them mercilessly, but the leader shows mercy, it reveals a character that is Christ-like, rooted in love. Being merciless reveals a lack of love.

Lord, reveal to me when I am merciless toward others. Help me to be more like you.

MEDITATION: Has anyone ever acted merciless toward you? It could have been a boss, a partner, a family member or a stranger. If so, how did you feel when it was happening?

THIRTY-FIVE

THIEVES

"Thieves, greedy people, drunkards, abusers, and swindlers—none of these will have a share in the Kingdom of God." (I Corinthian 6: 10)

If we were to survey people in the workplace, both employees and employers, and asked them if they considered themselves to be a "thief," all would likely say "no." If we were to ask these same people how many of them liked thieves, most likely many would answer with an adamant "no." Yet, today thievery in the workplace accounts for billions and billions of dollars stolen.

Thievery in the insurance industry by homeowners is responsible for a great part of the cost of our premiums. How can it be that we do not like thieves, yet we commit theft every day? Is it because we have come to rationalize and loosely define what is theft? Is the value of what is taken what defines theft? If this is so, then an act of theft is very different for a secretary who takes office supplies for her or his child, from that of a CEO of a multi-million conglomerate.

It is interesting to note that the value of office supplies taken by employees for their children at the beginning of their school year

119

amounts to millions of dollars, and the value of time spent by employees answering personal e-mails and surfing the Internet for personal reasons amounts of millions of dollars in lost revenues. The same is true of the value of time stolen from our families engaged in personal and selfish activities. It is sad to know that the average father spends less than 6 minutes a day of one-on-one time with his children, but that same father will spend hours watching television.

Theft cannot be defined by culture. Theft is any time we take something from someone that does not belong to us. That something is not limited to money; that something can be time and love. Just as Caesar told His disciples to give to God what belonged to God and to Caesar what belonged to Caesar, we must place emphasis on not taking what is not ours, and giving to others what belongs to them, especially when that something is love.

Lord, convict me whenever I am taking what does not belong to me!

MEDITATION: Have you thought on how culture has influenced our definition of theft?

Jorge L. Valdés, Ph.D. *in Collaboration with Anthony Petrucci*

SEVEN POSITIVE

ATTITUDES

Jorge L. Valdés, Ph.D. *in Collaboration with Anthony Petrucci*

THIRTY-SIX

FAITHFUL

"But Ruth replied, 'Don't urge me to leave you or to turn back from you. Where you go I will go, and where you stay I will stay. Your people will be my people and your God my God. Where you die, I will die, and there I will be buried. May the LORD deal with me, be it ever so severely, if even death separates you and me.' When Naomi realized that Ruth was determined to go with her, she stopped urging her." (Ruth 1:16-18)

Ruth was faithful to her mother-in-law Naomi, committing to travel with her and stay with her, even claiming, "Your people will be my people, and your God my God." This determination to go with Naomi revealed Ruth's faithfulness. Ruth was essentially saying that, no matter how difficult things get, she was sticking with her mother-in-law.

How great would it be to have employees at your company who have this same level of commitment? An increasing number of people in the corporate world are embracing "mindfulness" (a form of meditation), but timeless wisdom reveals that the true secret ingredient to a life well-lived is faithfulness.

This faithfulness likely seems odd or extremely rare in the 21st century. Today, most people would be repulsed by an expectation to be so utterly faithful. Today, people want to go their own way, do their own thing and not be tied to anyone. They don't want responsibility, accountability or integrity. They don't want to be tied down to a spouse, a family member or an employer. They want to be with who they want to be with and then change at the drop of a hat. They don't want to be inconvenienced. They are fine with being faithless. Being faithful is too hard, too serious and too demanding for them. They reject the notion that you are to work at your job as if you are working for God himself.

The idea of being faithful to a spouse in marriage almost seems anachronistic today as well. Traditionally, monogamy was the expectation and the standard for marriage. However, in today's society, many people see faithfulness as boring, unsuitable and nearly impossible. To be faithful means to choose not to fall into temptation at the workplace with a co-worker; it means to bypass opportunities for infidelity at a drunken company party; it means choosing to be faithful to God before choosing to willfully be faithless. To be faithful is to honor marriage vows and to honor promises to God as part of a relationship with the Creator. To be faithful is to keep committed, even when it's tough. Faithfulness must be tested in the fire of inconvenience.

Compare the actions of a churchgoer, a businessman and a narco. A churchgoer attends church every week but is having an affair with a young lady in the choir. A businessman is keeping his "perfect" image pristine in order to sell more products, but he forgets about each customer as soon as they sign the contract. A narco discovers a partner is in trouble and, instead of protecting himself, he launches into a dangerous situation to rescue his partner. Which one is more faithful?

To be faithful is to maintain a commitment and to turn it into action, even if it puts your life or your comfort in danger.

Lord, teach me to be faithful to you, to my family and to my business associates, so they may see the work you are doing in my heart to make me a trustworthy person whom others can depend on because of my faithfulness.

MEDITATION: What do you think of a person who is faithful? How faithful have you been to others?

Jorge L. Valdés, Ph.D. *in Collaboration with Anthony Petrucci*

THIRTY-SEVEN

HOPEFUL

"Pharaoh said to Joseph, 'I had a dream, and no one can interpret it. But I have heard it said of you that when you hear a dream you can interpret it.' 'I cannot do it,' Joseph replied to Pharaoh, 'but God will give Pharaoh the answer he desires.'" (Genesis 41: 15-16)

When Joseph told Pharaoh that "God will give Pharaoh the answer he desires," Joseph was being hopeful. He had made a choice to put his faith in God, and his faith fueled a staunch belief that God would show up in spirit and deliver the interpretation of the dream. Joseph's hope was in his God.

When a CEO says that his company will meet quarterly earnings next quarter, he is being hopeful. He is speaking authoritatively into the future of the company. Like Joseph, he has a conviction and he makes a choice to speak positively about his company.

As soon as Joseph said, "God will," he was expressing hope. He did not know 100% if God would deliver the dream interpretation. There are many instances in the Bible when a believer was expecting God to do something, but God either delayed or answered a prayer differently or was silent. But as soon as Joseph said, "God will," he was speaking hope and expectation into the atmosphere. His hope was not a modern-day "well, I hope it works out well, so we'll see" type of hedging-your-bets hope. No, Joseph's hope was rooted in conviction and an inner reality that God is faithful.

The story of Joseph is fascinating. Here was a young man who was sold into slavery by his brothers, nearly seduced by Potipher's wife if not for escaping, yet accused of attempted rape and thrown in prison. He had many reasons to resent God, curse God and be very negative. However, Joseph responded to Pharaoh with a hopeful response about how God is able to give dream interpretations.

As a professional in the business world, you have gone through difficulties in your career. You have reasons to be resentful and negative. But you have a hope deep in your soul, even if sometimes it only seems like a glimmer. You are smart to cultivate and protect this hope. You know that all things are possible.

No matter what you are going through in life, you can be hopeful because you are connected to the One who is the source of hope.

Lord, I thank you for being my hope and making me hopeful about tomorrow. Circumstances don't determine if I am hopeful or not. I know you work all things for good for those who love you and are called according to your purpose.

Jorge L. Valdés, Ph.D. *in Collaboration with Anthony Petrucci*

MEDITATION: What makes you hopeful today? Is your hope always tied directly to circumstances? What do you think about Joseph's hope in the book of Genesis? Joseph had spent years in slavery and jail. He certainly had legitimate reasons to be hopeless.

THIRTY-EIGHT
DUTY

"In the same way when you obey me you should say we are not worthy of praise we are servants who have simply done our duty." (Luke 17: 10)

In his book *A Promise Kept*, Robertson McQuilkin writes: "The decision to come to Columbia University was the most difficult I have had to make, the decision to leave 22 years later, though painful, was one of the easiest. . . Let me explain. My dear wife, Muriel, has been in failing mental health for about 12 years. So far, I have been able to carry both her ever-growing needs and my leadership responsibility at Columbia. But recently it has become apparent that Muriel is content most of the times she is with me and almost none of the time I am away from her. It is not just 'discontent.' She is filled with fear - even terror - when she has lost me and always goes in search of me when I leave home. So it clear to me that she needs me now full-time. . . The decision was made, in a way, 42 years ago when I promised to care for Muriel 'in sickness and in health . . . till death do us part.' So as I told my students and faculty, as a man of my word, integrity has something to do with it. But so does fairness. Duty, however, can be grim and stoic. I do not have to care for Muriel, I get to! It is a high honor to care for so wonderful a person."

It is interesting to observe how many "trusted, life-long friends-wise and godly" urged McQuilkin to institutionalize his wife for the sake of the Kingdom of God. After all, they suggested, she would not know the difference. Yet his decision to forsake all to fulfill his vow is quite amazing, especially in a world where words like "duty" and "honor" have been replaced by words such as "responsibility," something we have the option to assume or delegate to others.

For a man who always believed that God was first and family second, McQuilkin could have easily shifted the responsibility for the care of his wife to others: "Should I put the kingdom of God first and, for the sake of Christ and the kingdom, arrange for institutionalization?" Putting the kingdom of God first meant honoring a vow he had made before God to his wife 42 years earlier.

Yet, for McQuilkin, it was not his responsibility to take care of his dying wife; it was his duty and, most importantly, his honor. As we traverse through a postmodern culture that teaches us to "look out for number one," it is easy to delegate many of our responsibilities, especially those that interfere with our comfort zone and for which there exist the possibility of great loss. But, if we are to change the face of a culture that breeds self-gratification and not sacrifice, we must reach back to those days when duty and honor were inseparable words. When it was our duty and honor to fulfill our vows and, conversely, the possibility of not doing so was not an option.

Lord, allow me to find great duty and honor in being a servant. Allow me to be different, and when faced with hard choices in a world which seeks self-fulfillment, allow me to find freedom not in responsibility, but in duty and honor.

MEDITATION: What is the difference to you between duty and honor and responsibility?

Jorge L. Valdés, Ph.D. *in Collaboration with Anthony Petrucci*

THIRTY-NINE

GRATEFUL

"And let the peace that comes from Christ rule in your hearts. For as members of one body you are all called to live in peace. And always be thankful." (Colossians 3: 15).

When we consider the word "thankful," especially in light of the above verse, it is easy for us to say that truly we are thankful people. We are thankful for all the blessings we receive during our lifetime; we are thankful when we receive a promotion in our workplace; for those of us who have owned our own business we are thankful when we close a major deal or when we have a particularly good month, and perhaps for many others of us we are thankful when on Friday we can pay payroll.

The bottom line is that it is all relevant. What I am grateful for is very different than what you are grateful for. It does not take much encouragement to get people to be thankful for their blessings. As a whole, people want to be grateful for what life provides for them. The difficulty does not lie in giving thanks for good times; the real difficulty lies in giving thanks when times are not just right.

Jorge L. Valdés, Ph.D. *in Collaboration with Anthony Petrucci*

The difficulty is when it seems that the world has closed in on us and has choked all the air out of us. Yet, when we read the verse above, it does not say to be thankful in good times or most of the time; it clearly says "always." This always includes difficult and painful moments.

How do we make sense of this? I believe the answer lies in how we define faith. Is faith something that is rational or irrational? Do we say that faith is blind and we most work hard to allow our faith to grow? There might be some validity to this. I believe that faith is totally rational. It is a simple process of believing that every word in the Bible is true.

Is the process of knowing that we can trust in God because throughout history He has proven to be trustworthy? Finally, is believing Him when He says: "I will never abandon you nor forsake you."

Lord, allow me to be thankful for the trials and tribulation you permit me to go through.

MEDITATION: Are you always thankful when hard times arrive?

Jorge L. Valdés, Ph.D. *in Collaboration with Anthony Petrucci*

FORTY

CONTRITION

"You do not desire a sacrifice, or I would offer one. You do not want a burnt offering. The sacrifice you desire is a broken spirit. You will not reject a broken and repentant heart, O God." (Psalm 51:16-17)

Many times we do others wrong and deep inside of us we are truly sorry for it. However, we wonder why it is that our conviction is not evident to those whom we have hurt. And why do we grow distant? This is even more critical when others have wronged us and they apologize, yet there seems to be no evidence of true remorse.

I suggest that the problem lies in our inability to understand contrition; therefore, what does it mean to be contrite? What does it mean to have a contrite heart? And is it possible to come clean without it? Finally, can we ever expect to be truly repentant when, in fact, we are not contrite about our actions?

The Encarta dictionary defines "contrition" as a deep and genuine feeling of guilt and remorse. A deep sense of shame over past sins and a firm resolve not to sin in the future. The English Thesaurus defines contrition as repentance, penitence, remorse, regret, sorrow and

Jorge L. Valdés, Ph.D. *in Collaboration with Anthony Petrucci*

apology. The list goes on and on and we can even break down further words such as sin, sorrow, and penitence, and, in the end, we would spend countless hours of debate and never reach any sort of agreement as to what the word really means.

Let us pause for a moment on Encarta's definition of a genuine feeling of guilt and remorse and consider it as precursors to the process of liberation by which we are delivered, restored and healed as we become transparent before Christ, family and those we have hurt. To be transparent, we must first look at our contrite heart, or, as Encarta would say, guilty and remorseful heart, and recognize that we have done wrong, and in doing so we have hurt those whom we love and have created a wall that prevents us from having an intimate relationship with our loved one and God.

What did it mean for me to have a contrite heart? Better yet, how did I even know that I needed to have a contrite heart and without it I would remain in bondage and thus unable to be transparent? For me, it was a process. It was not some instantaneous conviction where I realized that I was this horrific sinner that needed to repent and fix all the wrong that I had done and make it all better with those I had hurt so much.

It was a process by which God convicted me of the fact that the daily choices I made in search of some mysterious meaning to life were mere satisfaction of personal selfish desires. It was the moment when I began to realize that these choices were separating me more and more from those I loved so much. It was the feeling that something was deeply wrong, and I had to fix it, yet I was not able.

Contrition is not real until we realize that we are lonely, desperate and unable to utter phrases such as: "I am hurting," "I am lonely," "I am scared," or "I am weak." It is hard to show a contrite heart because society has taught us to be macho, hide our need to be dependent, be an individual, and, when the load becomes too heavy to carry any longer, just crumble and fall. But true repentance and healing cannot occur until we become contrite.

Lord, allow my contrite heart to be so transparent that liberation can occur.

MEDITATION: Have you ever wondered why others do not seem to think you are truly sorry? Why the wounds of our pain never heal?

FORTY-ONE

JOYFUL

"But they were childless because Elizabeth was not able to conceive, and they were both very old....Then an angel of the Lord appeared to him...said to him: 'Do not be afraid, Zechariah; your prayer has been heard. Your wife Elizabeth will bear you a son, and you are to call him John. He will be a joy and delight to you, and many will rejoice because of his birth...'"

(Luke 1:7, 11-14)

Zechariah and his wife Elizabeth had not been able to have a child, but just when it looked like they were too old, then Elizabeth became pregnant and gave birth to special boy, a child of promise. The shift from being infertile to becoming pregnant and giving birth is a joyful experience. In this case, the angel told Zechariah declared that the child "will be a joy and delight to you." There is something about joy that lifts the human spirit.

In the business world, just when it looks like your business will crumble or not make it another week without defaulting on payroll obligations, a surprise thing happens. New customers come in. Business starts to boom. Your spirit is lifted. You start to sense that you are going to be okay. You allow yourself to be joyful. What relief!

Jorge L. Valdés, Ph.D. *in Collaboration with Anthony Petrucci*

Seeing a prayer answered, especially after a long wait, can be incredibly uplifting. You may have waited for your business to start doing well financially. You may have been waiting and praying for a big contract. You may have been patient trying to work through a conflict. Whatever has been the desire of your heart, when you receive it, you experience joy. It has the power to push back the effect of disappointment, sadness and fatigue. Joy energizes you.

By being joyful also goes beyond an experience of having a desire fulfilled. It is also an attitude that you can choose to practice every day, no matter what the circumstance is. When you look within yourself and your relationship with God, you can find reasons to be joyful today, even if you are still waiting for an answer to a prayer or for certain challenges to be resolved, for example, at work with colleagues.

Happiness is more temporary. If your company makes a higher-than-expected profit this quarter, you're happy. But joy runs at a deeper level of the soul and spirit. Joy comes out of an inner knowing that you are not alone in the universe and that you are loved to the point of where your prayers are answered for the right reasons at the right time, even if not on your timeline. When joy floods your spirit (inner person), it affects everything in your life, including your career, and you can sustain it by faith.

Choosing to be joyful renews the soul. It gives you a bounce in your step, and people will see it at your job. It clears your mind and strengthens you to focus on what is most important, rather than having a pity party for yourself. You can always find a reason to be joyful.

Lord, I want to experience deeper and richer reservoirs of your joy. Strengthen me to choose to be joyful, even in the face of challenges and adversities.

MEDITATION: What do you see as the differences between happiness and joy? What has made you truly joyful in life? What do you see as the relationship between joy and faith?

Jorge L. Valdés, Ph.D. *in Collaboration with Anthony Petrucci*

FORTY-TWO

TRANSPARENT

"Yes, we are fully confident, and we would rather be away from these earthly bodies, for then we will be at home with the Lord." (2 Corinthians 5:8)

Often we talk about transparency and somehow we want the world to believe that we are transparent people who have nothing to hide and are always predictable. Yet, in reality, this is so far from the truth, and even though we aspire to be transparent, I suggest that we simply do not understand what the word really means; and to many of us the word implies a certain state of vulnerability, which by no means can be comfortable.

In today's society we guard our privacy at all cost, and at the same time it seems that we have this deep hunger that yearns for intimacy; we yearn to be intimate with our spouses, our children, our co-workers, yet it seems we are unable to achieve this and every day we grow more distant. We are social, but we poor at being intimate. It is evident that a conflict exists between our desire to be private and our desire for intimacy.

Jorge L. Valdés, Ph.D. *in Collaboration with Anthony Petrucci*

I want to suggest that we look at transparency not as a vulnerable state to be avoided at all cost, but as a posture that provides a safe place for us and those whom we love to find intimacy and healing, especially when our distance is a result of inflicted pain. What does this form of transparency mean? Does it mean we confess our sins to the entire world and risk being judged and condemned? That might be the case for some, as it was for me, but, in reality, not. Being transparent means that we allow ourselves to be seen as He sees us: transparent in order to provide a safe place for loved ones to enter.

For me, being transparent was writing a book and revealing the hidden skeletons which haunted me; telling my loved ones, and the world things that I rather had kept hidden in the deepest crevices of my soul, and making it so transparent that my brokenness was evident to all. My urgency to be transparent was that moment of conviction and realization that, if Jesus was going to do a work in my life and fill that void deep within me, I had to come clean and be transparent.

Being transparent does not mean that the pain deep within us disappears right away and never affects us again; in fact, this may never happen to many of us. What it does mean is that now we have a chance to find healing and, if we have a chance, then our children and loved ones have a chance, and together we can begin to build a stronger foundation for our lives. It is very difficult to be transparent to the world and expose ourselves to pain. Yet, the greatest pain is the pain we inflict on ourselves and others when we continue to hold to those chains that bind us all.

Lord, allow me to be transparent so that I can be truly intimate with you and my loved ones.

MEDITATION: Are you transparent before your loved ones, and, if so, how much emotional intimacy and spiritual intimacy do you have with them?

Jorge L. Valdés, Ph.D. *in Collaboration with Anthony Petrucci*

SEVEN STATES

OF BEING

Jorge L. Valdés, Ph.D. *in Collaboration with Anthony Petrucci*

FORTY-THREE

BELIEF

"Your word is a lamp for my feet and a light for my path. I've promised it once, and I'll promise it again: I will obey your wonderful laws . . . Lord, accept my grateful thanks and teach me your law. My life constantly hangs in the balance, but I will not stop obeying your law. . . Your decrees are my treasure; they are truly my heart's delight. I am determined to keep your principles, even forever, to the very end." (Psalm 119: 105-109, 111-112)

One look at the terrain of the land of Palestine and one can imagine how difficult it was to traverse the land at night. When a person traveled at night, he literally attached a candleholder to his sandals. The light from the candle would illuminate a small area of his path. Yet, with this limited amount of light, that person was able to take one step at a time with the assurance that he would not stumble or fall.

When the Psalmist writes, "your word is a lamp unto my feet," the reader, or listener, could visualize God's Word as sufficient to help him to take that next step. The Word was only intended for that next step. The guarantee was that, if that person adhered to God's Word, one step at a time, that person would not stumble.

Jorge L. Valdés, Ph.D. *in Collaboration with Anthony Petrucci*

Marion Wade, founder of ServiceMaster, was known for saying: "If you do not live it, you do not believe it." This saying has a direct correlation to our behavior in the workplace as well as outside the workplace. We consistently tell people what we believe, yet our actions are short of a clear manifestation of those beliefs. For us who call ourselves Christians, we seem to easily separate our faith from our daily behavior. We go to Church most of the time; yes, sometimes we even attend Bible studies. And, when things are going wonderfully well, we shine as exemplary citizens. But, when times become difficult, when our jobs do not seem to be all that we want them to be, when affliction settles in, and when our children go astray, we quickly put our faith on the shelf and take matters into our own hands, most of the time to make them worse.

Your Word is a lamp unto my feet. If we grasp the principle, this verse provides and clings to God's revealed Word as a basis for our next decision today, not tomorrow, not next year. Then, we can take that step with firmness and conviction, believing that God's Word will not fail us. When we do this, our lives will clearly demonstrate what we truly believe. Then, and only then, the world will be able to say that person truly lives what he/she believes. Our lives must be a clear reflection of what we believe.

Lord, allow me to walk one step at a time with you. And allow that walk to be a witness of what I believe.

MEDITATION: Is God's Word a light unto your feet?

144

FORTY-FOUR
MANIPULATIVE

"Jezebel his wife said, 'Is this how you act as king over Israel? Get up and eat! Cheer up. I'll get you the vineyard of Naboth the Jezreelite.' So she wrote letters in Ahab's name, placed his seal on them, and sent them to the elders and nobles who lived in Naboth's city with him.

In those letters she wrote: 'Proclaim a day of fasting and seat Naboth in a prominent place among the people. But seat two scoundrels opposite him and have them bring charges that he has cursed both God and the king. Then take him out and stone him to death.'" (1 Kings 21:7-10)

The name "Jezebel" is generally associated with manipulative, conniving behavior. Even in modern society, people describe a manipulative person as "a Jezebel." In the Old Testament, Jezebel was a strong-willed character who would do whatever it takes to get her way. She would lie, cheat, steal, flatter and, yes, manipulate. She did not see anything wrong with it. It was just her way to get what she desired. She was always looking out for herself and saw people and circumstances as subject to her desires.

In the story shared in the scripture above, Jezebel pretended to be her husband by issuing a decree and manipulated the circumstances to

Jorge L. Valdés, Ph.D. *in Collaboration with Anthony Petrucci*

get rid of Naboth, so that she and her husband could more easily acquire Naboth's vineyard. She came up with a scheme and executed on it, with no regard for honesty, empathy or respect. She was the consummate manipulator.

How many people in the workplace use Jezebel-like schemes to get their way? In the corporate world, perception is considered "reality." So when a person of little to no integrity gets a hold in the workplace, he or she can be very manipulative and, therefore, destructive. Outcomes are being affected by less than honorable means and by hidden agendas, just as Jezebel had a hidden agenda.

We aren't going to change the business world overnight, and there will always be manipulators in the workplace, but ancient wisdom, as found in the Scriptures, challenges leaders to not choose to be manipulative, but rather to lead with compassion, truth, integrity, honor and love. Manipulation is a low form of leadership. It involves coercion, half-truths, deception and a controlling spirit.

What is interesting about the Jezebel character in the book of 1 Kings is that part of her agenda was to silence the prophets, who were telling the truth. The antidote to Jezebel-like manipulative behavior is to raise the stakes on truth and drive a higher degree of transparency and truth-telling. This exposes the Jezebel mindset. In the workplace, you need to speak the truth and not be silenced about your moral values.

Lord, reveal to me any ways that I am being manipulative myself and don't recognize it; help me to change. Guide me to elevate my leadership to be committed to transparency and truth. Open my eyes to when others are being manipulative and I need to either confront it or steer clear of it.

MEDITATION: Have you ever known anyone who exhibited manipulative behavior? How do you know what manipulation is? How does it make you feel?

FORTY-FIVE

COMING CLEAN

"So put away all falsehood and tell your neighbor the truth."

(Ephesians 4: 25)

As discussed in the devotional on lying, "The Summer of Mistrust" would begin with the fall of Enron, which cost investors over 60 billion dollars and wipe out millions of Americans' retirement.

The result of such chaos is that Americans have no confidence that our leaders in various professions would consistently make morally appropriate decisions in their workplace. This paints a very dim picture of ethics in today's workplace. Often times we take a defeated attitude and wonder who are we to change the culture of such giants of corporate America? Or how are we able to change things?

First, let us recognize that our nation was not built by mega-companies where truth seems to be relative and, at times, non-existent. America was built by the simple man/woman who started a small business, and its identity did not lie in the product being sold but in the person behind that product. It was a time where our "yes" was "yes" and our "no" was "no"; a time when credit was based on a handshake

Jorge L. Valdés, Ph.D. *in Collaboration with Anthony Petrucci*

and not a credit report. A handshake was the only "document" needed to execute a contract. Once we realize this, then the question becomes how do we rebuild an American workplace where our gift to future generations would be the value of truth?

I believe that to rebuild something, whether it is an automobile, an airplane or broken body, we must go back to its foundation. To rebuild a nation where our words mean absolutely nothing and attorneys are more important than a handshake, we must begin with repentance and confession. We have harmed many throughout our work life. These acts might not be in the scale of Enron, Adelphia or Martha Stewart; nevertheless, they are wrong choices we made which have hurt and deceived somebody. We can leave it at that and hope all gets well one day or we can take a bold step and "Come Clean."

When we come clean with those whom we have hurt, deceived or cheated, we take the first step in re-establishing trust. When we come clean about our actions and show a contrite heart, it sets the stage for those whom we have hurt and with those whom we come in contact with to know that there is a convicting element in us that is telling us to repent. If it seems that easy, why has our actions gone silent for so long? Mainly because in a society that promotes individualism and self-achievement at any cost, any expression of pain and repentance is immediately judged as weakness; therefore, how does all this work? How can we find freedom in coming clean?

Jorge L. Valdés, Ph.D. *in Collaboration with Anthony Petrucci*

The answer begins with God's instruction for us to confess our sins one to another. It seems amazingly easy, and at the same time, it is insurmountably hard. Yet, if we are to experience a change in our lives, the first step is admit that in and of myself I am incapable of change and, therefore, I no longer need to ask those around me to pray for my distant aunt who has a cold or lost a job or some other superficial prayer we are so good at making. I am now free to look at you and tell you that my battle is a daily battle. I can do this because by confessing our sins one to another, we then create a safe place for expression and healing; this is freedom.

Freedom begins with surrendering to God and admitting that individualism is not the answer, and the day we come clean we are liberated because, for one, our secrets no longer hold us captive. Second, once we are transparent with our lives with those whom we love, then we create a safe place for healing to take place and for real intimacy to occur.

Lord, give me the strength to come clean with those whom I need to come clean.

MEDITATION: Is there some hidden act within your heart that you are being convicted about and know that you have to come clean with?

Jorge L. Valdés, Ph.D. *in Collaboration with Anthony Petrucci*

FORTY-SIX

STAYING CLEAN

"It is God's will that you should be sanctified: that you should avoid sexual immorality; that each of you should learn to control your own body in a way that is holy and honorable, not in passionate lust like the pagans, who do not know God; and that in this matter no one should wrong or take advantage of a brother or sister." (1 Thessalonians 4:3-6)

It is one thing to come clean and then it's another thing to stay clean. A person can come clean, admit everything, be transparent and express good intentions, but still fall soon afterward right back into addictions, immorality and hedonism. The journey of staying clean is a life-long commitment to continue to work on yourself, finding healing for the deep hurts and thinking patterns that drive you to fall back into your old ways.

Scriptures talks about self-control. This is not a popular concept in the 21st century, but it's vital for living a life that is pleasing to God. Because God is pure himself and is in relationship with you, he doesn't want anything sinful to hold you back or block your relationship with him.

Jorge L. Valdés, Ph.D. *in Collaboration with Anthony Petrucci*

He is not trying to ruin your "fun." He is calling you to staying clean – which, in church circles, is called sanctification – because he wants you to receive his best and not harm yourself by falling into the traps of lust and sexual immorality. Only then can you be truly joyful and have fun that is free of guilt and shame.

Staying clean require guts, grit and gusto. It doesn't just happen – not in a fallen world that continually throws temptations at you, trying to appeal to the broken places in you to violate God's guidelines, the way a football player ignores his coach's guidance, only to get hammered by the other team, lose the ball, lose the game and be down and out for the count.

Staying clean helps you in business. You are more focused, more stable, more dependable and more trustworthy. An organization knows they can trust you because you do deny yourself selfish pleasures for the sake of doing what is right. This translates into putting your ego aside to do what is best and what is right for your company.

In order to stay clean, you need to adopt a mindset that is tough enough to keep you on the straight and narrow path, living in freedom from your addictions. It involves a process steeped in transparency, contrition, authenticity and self-control. Many people who come clean and, subsequently, stay clean have hit rock bottom in their lives, but the opportunity exists for you to stay clean proactively. And this is a message that young people need to hear, for many of them don't even know what "clean" means. For young people, in particular, staying

Jorge L. Valdés, Ph.D. *in Collaboration with Anthony Petrucci*

clean equates to staying at your best and staying in freedom, rather than in the terrible bondage of addictions.

Lord, just as you help me to come clean about my life, I ask you to strengthen me to stay clean each and every day.

MEDITATION: What do I need to do to stay clean? What parameters do I need to adhere to in my life? Where am I weak and how can I protect myself from missteps?

Jorge L. Valdés, Ph.D. *in Collaboration with Anthony Petrucci*

FORTY-SEVEN
SECURITY

"Some nations boast of their armies and weapons but we boast in the Lord our God. Those nations will fall and collapse, but we will rise up and stand firm." (Psalm 20: 7-8)

The United States military budget is said to exceed the combined military budget of more than 80 percent of all the combined budgets of other nations. There is absolutely no doubt in anyone's mind that America is the only standing world power, and militarily no other nation can stand against us. Yet, as we look at our nation's youth, we find a very chaotic nation, a nation that consumes over 60 percent of the world's production of narcotics. A nation where 88,000 teenage girls will get pregnant in the next thirty days; 3,250,000 teenagers will consume drugs in the same thirty days; and a nation where every 17 seconds a teenager attempts suicide. All the statistics point to not a world power, but a sick nation; why?

I suggest that the reason for the above lies in our concept of security. We are consumed with finding security in the stock market, in our workplace, in a retirement account, and in our wealth; yet, we fail to realize that each and every one of these are all temporal. At any given

Jorge L. Valdés, Ph.D. *in Collaboration with Anthony Petrucci*

moment in life, most of us have experienced the loss of something we thought was much secured. We have lost jobs, seen the stock market crash, lost homes and some have lost their greatest asset: their children.

We find security in everything the world has to offer, and at times pay dearly for it. We sacrifice our families for our jobs; we sacrifice our health to accumulate wealth, only to find that sooner or later we have to spend that wealth to recuperate our health. The experience of seeing thousands of hard-working Americans lose their entire retirement has taught America that even that which seems very secure can disappear in the blink of an eye.

Our verse today teaches us that our only security lies in our dependence with our Creator. We spend our entire lives trying to figure out the meaning to our life, yet how can we know what we were created for if we did not create ourselves? Only a Creator knows what he/she created something for. Therefore, as we go through life, it will serve us well to seek God's face not only for our security but also for the meaning to our lives. Then, and only then, are we able to experience true security.

Lord, give me a hunger for your word so that I can truly know what I was created for, and then I will be able to find meaning to my life.

MEDITATION: Take an inventory of your life and ask yourself where and in what you find your security.

FORTY-EIGHT

PRAYER

"The Lord said, 'Go over to Straight Street, to the house of Judas. When you arrive, ask for Saul of Tarsus. He is praying to me right now. 2 I have shown him a vision of a man named Ananias coming in and laying his hands on him so that he can see again." (Acts 9: 11-12).

There is probably not a more out-of-place word in today's workplace and culture than the word "prayer." We have seen Supreme Court cases banning prayer from schools; years ago, the University of Georgia football coach Mark Richt had come under attack for having prayer before games. And if a company has regular scheduled prayer time, that company is risking legal litigation. Yet, during times of hardship and great tribulation, even those who call themselves atheists will pray to God for help.

It is interesting, as we read the above passage, that, when the Lord instructs Ananias to go and lay hands on Paul, Jesus tells us that Paul was praying. Paul had just been blinded by Christ... and his first reaction was not to cry or have some type of a nervous attack. No, he begins to pray; he humbles himself, drops to his knees and prays. Out

Jorge L. Valdés, Ph.D. *in Collaboration with Anthony Petrucci*

of the hundreds of passages that refer to prayer, this passage has the greatest impact on me.

It impacts me because somehow I want to learn to live a life that, when any circumstance in my life occurs, my first reaction is to go into prayer. Prayer is an exercise of surrendering our will to a greater will. It is the act of worship where we come before our Creator, admitting that we need His guidance and love to get us by. As humans, we have no problem knowing the difference between right and wrong; our struggle lies in finding the will to do what is right; only through prayer and submission are we able to find this will.

As I look back at two hurricanes Charley and Frances that devastated the state of Florida, and hurricane Ivan that threatened to inflict its own fury, I wonder how many people prayed before they boarded up their homes. I wonder how many of us pray before we react to some bad news, or circumstance; I wonder how many of us believe that the God we pray to really cares and will answer our prayer. In the Gospel of Mark 11: 24-25, Jesus places great emphasis on believing as we ask.

Finally, as we pray, how many of us are praying to our Father? It is critical to realize that, if some child asks a complete stranger for something he/she desires, chances are that most of the time they will not get what they are asking for; after all, is it not reasonable to assume that our only responsibility is to our own children? The same is true with our Father; it is safe to assume that many of us whose prayers are not answered are due to the fact that we have not made Him our Father.

Lord, teach me to live a life of prayer where I wake up with prayer on my mind and go to sleep praying.

MEDITATION: During times of crisis, is prayer your first response? If not, why not?

Jorge L. Valdés, Ph.D. *in Collaboration with Anthony Petrucci*

FORTY-NINE

EQUITY

"Tell all the nations that the Lord is king. The world is firmly established and cannot be shaken. He will judge all peoples fairly." (Psalm 96: 10).

"Equity," like the word "Justice," is a term that is very difficult to understand and make sense of. As we look around our world and see all the inequity that exists, how then do we make sense of the fact that God tells us that He will judge all people fairly when, in fact, many times a quick glance reveals that life is anything but fair?

Looking back during the times in which I rejected any notion of the existence of God, my defense always centered on equity. I would ask those who insisted on the existence of God: How can there be a God who is "love" when we see the wicked prosper?; when we see innocent children die every day?; when good, decent couples cannot have babies, yet there are babies born in crack houses every day? Why would God provide life in a crack house if, in fact, it is true that only He gives life? What kind of a wicked God is one who closes the womb of a decent woman and opens the one of a crack addict?

Jorge L. Valdés, Ph.D. *in Collaboration with Anthony Petrucci*

How do we correlate the fact that decent, hard-working single mothers with great faith pray and pray for God to protect their children from the horrors surrounding their neighborhoods and yet a drive-by shooting takes these innocent children's lives? Why is it that in our workplace we often see those who try to conduct their lives ethically don't get ahead and yet those who cheat and lie seem to be the ones that prosper? These are hard questions to which I could not find any answers until I discovered God's equity.

As human beings, we reduce issues of equity to comparisons between these people and those people, this situation against that situation; often reducing it to "who behaves how during which period of time." When we simplify God's equity and judge it according to our system of understanding, we simply miss out on God's true equity.

God's true equity is expressed not in that we receive what we deserve but in that in His infinite wisdom He provided humanity with His Son; not that we be judged and condemned but that we would be redeemed and sanctified.

God's equity is exemplified at Calvary as forgiveness and grace; where a condemned humanity is redeemed and made equal in Christ. Where a condemned humanity is not judged and sentenced but loved and set free. In our humanity we understand God's view of equity when we love those who are most unlovable; when we join in solidarity with those who are oppressed and abused. We might never make sense or

Jorge L. Valdés, Ph.D. *in Collaboration with Anthony Petrucci*

even comprehend God's equity, but we surely can experience it when we do the above.

Lord, allow me to understand your equity as I love those who are difficult to love.

MEDITATION: Have you considered God's equity?

Jorge L. Valdés, Ph.D. *in Collaboration with Anthony Petrucci*

FIFTY

PERCEPTION

"Now we see things imperfectly as in a poor mirror, but then we will see everything with perfect clarity. All that I know now is partial and incomplete, but then I will know everything completely, just as God knows me now." (I Corinthians 13: 11-12)

In his bestseller book *The 7 habits of Highly Effective People* , Stephen R. Covey writes: "He was doing poorly academically; he didn't even know how to follow the instructions on the tests. . . Socially he was immature, often embarrassing those closest to him. Athletically, he was small, skinny, and uncoordinated . . . Others would laugh at him."

Covey struggles with the perception that his son was "basically inadequate, somehow behind" until he and his wife realized that what they were doing to address these struggles that they perceived his son to be having was not in harmony with the ways they "really saw him."

For Covey, the realization came when he dwelt in how perceptions are formed. He concludes that when we realize how embedded our perceptions are, we realize that, as we look at the world around us, it is

Jorge L. Valdés, Ph.D. *in Collaboration with Anthony Petrucci*

critical to note that the lens through which we look at our particular world is as important as the world we see. In fact, the lens we look through is what defines the world we see.

As the writer to Corinthians deals with his inability to comprehend God's ways, he comes to the realization that his lens is foggy. It is only when he looks at his circumstances through God's eyes that the picture then becomes clear. I often struggle with the many "whys?" of our everyday life. Why do innocent children get hurt? Why are good people unable to bear children when there are babies born every day in crack houses? Why do bad things happen to me now that I am serving God and seeking His face daily when these things did not happen when I was a bad person? Why do many children go hungry every day in the world when in America most of us are in a diet?

These seem to be hard questions with no evident answers until we look at them through God's eyes. It is not until the moment we realize that our worldview has been shaped by a faulty, foggy lens that we are able to put on a new lens that will give us very clear vision. If we are color blind, it does not matter how often we look at colors, all we will see is gray. Until we look at our circumstances and the world around us through God's eyes, we will always see gray.

Lord, allow me to reshape the lens through which I see the world as I look at the world through your eyes.

Jorge L. Valdés, Ph.D. *in Collaboration with Anthony Petrucci*

MEDITATION: Through what lens have you been looking at the world?

Jorge L. Valdés, Ph.D. *in Collaboration with Anthony Petrucci*

FIFTY-ONE
HONORABLE

[18] His mother Mary was pledged to be married to Joseph, but before they came together, she was found to be pregnant through the Holy Spirit. ...an angel of the Lord appeared to him in a dream and said, 'Joseph son of David, do not be afraid to take Mary home as your wife, because what is conceived in her is from the Holy Spirit...' When Joseph woke up, he did what the angel of the Lord had commanded him and took Mary home as his wife."

(Matthew 1:18, 20, 24)

In the culture in which Jesus' parents Joseph and Mary lived, it was perfectly acceptable for a man to expose a woman who was pregnant outside of wedlock and to put her away or even stone her. Such a thing as unfaithfulness brought shame upon a husband-to-be, and it was practically a man's right to deal harshly with a woman who is perceived as disloyal, immoral and dishonorable.

In other words, it was encouraged in the culture of the day to expose the woman to disgrace, just as cultures in a workplace today encourage people to judge others, throw verbal "stones" and insults at colleagues to tear them down, and spread gossip about others, as if the area around

Jorge L. Valdés, Ph.D. *in Collaboration with Anthony Petrucci*

a water cooler at an office in the 21st century is a public square of workplace "disgrace."

When Joseph found out that Mary was pregnant before they had gotten married, he did not want to expose her to public disgrace. Even though he was a man faithful to the law and the appearance of Mary breaking the religious law justified any disciplinary action against her, he was gentle and gracious toward her. He did not want to make a public spectacle of her. He did not want to spread gossip about her or rip her apart verbally behind her back with others. He was going to deal with the serious issue privately, as to cover her and treat her honorably, even though he was hurt and confused.

Likewise, in the workplaces of today, when a manager is gracious toward an employee who is "perceived" as having made a mistake, the manager is viewed as honorable. He deals with the matter privately – without exposing the employee to disgrace among colleagues in the office. He is honorable for maintaining his high standards while preserving the honor and respect of the other person, just as Joseph was preserving the honor of Mary, the mother of Jesus.

If companies had more "honorable managers" working for them, how different would the corporate world be today?

Going back to the story in the Scriptures, when Joseph had a dream in which he learned that Mary was pregnant because of God (the immaculate conception), he chose to believe what the angel had told

Jorge L. Valdés, Ph.D. *in Collaboration with Anthony Petrucci*

him in the dream. He made the decision to be an honorable husband and believe his wife and to treat her with love and care, still marrying her and waiting until after Jesus was born to consummate the marriage. What Joseph did was worthy of honor. In contrast, if he had ditched Mary, exposed her to public disgrace or had her stoned for sex outside marriage, would the world have ever known Jesus Christ? The honorable behavior and decisions of one man, Joseph, made the difference for the next two thousand years.

In the workplace, you can have that kind of impact on a person's life, refusing to gossip about a co-worker in the office, but treating them with respect and honor, and consistently showing honor, which ultimately reflects back on you as an honorable person. It may look like a co-worker or staff member has faltered, even egregiously. But to be honorable is to cover the person with honor (your own honor) and to give them a chance to explain and be treated fairly; there may be more in the situation than it appears. Just ask Joseph and Mary! To be honorable is to be the bigger person, overlooking an offense or treating someone respectfully, no matter what.

Lord, I ask you to help me to treat others honorably and for me to learn from you in your Word on how I can be a more honorable person.

MEDITATION: Can you think of specific times when you acted honorably and, on the flip side, when you did not act honorably? To you, what is the difference between being honorable and not being honorable? How do you think it relates to where you work?

Jorge L. Valdés, Ph.D. *in Collaboration with Anthony Petrucci*

FIFTY-TWO

MORALITY

"Even when Gentiles, who do not have God's written law, instinctively follow what the law says, they show that in their hearts they know right from wrong." (Romans 2: 14)

According to the author of the letter to the Romans, every human being has a sense of what is right and what is wrong, aside from any prescribed religious ordinance, almost as if subscribing to the theory that religion has no direct bearing on morality. Yet, in today's postmodern society, where a majority of the population is seeking some form of spirituality, we might benefit from visiting C.S. Lewis' exposition on the religious foundation of ethics: in his opening chapter of Mere Christianity, Lewis suggests that, when people argue about moral issues such as: what you did is wrong, or you did me wrong, they act as if they know what is right and what is wrong. "Quarreling means trying to show that the other man is in the wrong. And there would be no sense in trying to do that unless you and he have some sort of agreement as to what Right and Wrong are."

According to Lewis, it would be very difficult for two individuals to observe that a certain athlete has committed a violation while competing in a certain sport unless these two individuals had the same knowledge of the rules pertinent to that sport; otherwise, the argument would have no basis and then right and wrong only becomes what is right and wrong for one of the individuals, without any consideration of what is right and wrong for the other individual.

This same principle applies to individuals in the workplace. As we are faced with making many moral decisions on a daily basis in the workplace, we must draw from an immutable source whose definition of what is right and wrong is accepted by all. As for Lewis, I suggest that this source be God's revealed Word in the Judeo-Christian writings.

For Lewis, the laws of science define the way things are; whereas, the laws of morality define the ways things ought to be. Yet, whereas for most societies, culture defines moral laws, for Lewis the only explanation of morality lies with God. For if culture defines what is right and wrong, then right and wrong are bound to space and time. What is right today... well, it must likely be wrong tomorrow, and what is wrong today might be right tomorrow. Whereas with God, what He has defined as right and wrong throughout time has remained a constant.

Lord, allow me to know your immutable truths so that my moral choices today would be my moral choices tomorrow.

Jorge L. Valdés, Ph.D. *in Collaboration with Anthony Petrucci*

MEDITATION: As others consider the moral choices you make every day in the workplace; can they observe a constant pattern or ever-changing pattern?

Jorge L. Valdés, Ph.D. *in Collaboration with Anthony Petrucci*